MORE

In-Depth Discussion of the Reasoning Activities in "Teaching Fractions and Ratios for Understanding"

Second Edition

MORE

In-Depth Discussion of the Reasoning Activities in "Teaching Fractions and Ratios for Understanding"

Second Edition

Susan J. Lamon
Marquette University

Routledge
Taylor & Francis Group
New York   London

First published by Lawrence Erlbaum Associates, Inc., Publishers
10 Industrial Avenue
Mahwah, New Jersey 07430

Reprinted 2009 by Routledge

270 Madison Avenue
New York, NY 10016

2 Park Square, Milton Park
Abingdon, Oxon OX14 4RN, UK

Cover design by Kathryn Houghtaling Lacey

Library of Congress Cataloging-in-Publication Data

More : In-depth discussion of the reasoning activities in "teaching fractions and
ratios for understanding" / Susan J. Lamon—2nd edition.

ISBN 0-8058-5211-5 (alk. paper).

Includes bibliographical references and index.

Copyright information for this volume can be obtained by contacting the Library of Congress.

10   9   8   7   6   5   4   3   2   1

For Bill

Contents

Preface

This resource book accompanies *Teaching Fractions and Ratios for Understanding: Essential Content Knowledge and Teaching Strategies for Teachers, Second Edition*. It was originally intended as a scaffold for adults who are reasoning their way through the fraction world for the first time. Reasoning after many years of rule-based computation presents a challenge to one's understanding, logical thinking, problem solving, and ability to communicate! *MORE* still serves that purpose. However, those who have used the previous edition will note several changes in organization and in content.

For ease of use, the supplementary activities have been moved so that they immediately follow the discussions of the activities from *Teaching Fractions and Ratios*. Instructors who use this book in pre-service teacher education courses have requested a set of activities without solutions. In response to their needs, solutions to the supplementary activities have been omitted. Nevertheless, because the number of activities in each chapter of the book has increased and complete discussions of all of them are provided in *MORE*, there will be ample opportunity to learn reasoning methods before removing the safety net.

MORE is not an answer key; good reasoning should produce correct answers, but the *process* is the goal. Everyone knows the conventional symbolic representations and algorithms for getting the correct answers. The purpose here is to demonstrate and to help you engage in powerful ways of thinking so that you can, in turn, enhance the mathematical education of your students.

Solutions are offered with this caveat: no solution should be taken as *the* way to think about a situation. *MORE* offers some suggestions, but no effort is made to exhaust all of the possibilities.

—*SJL*

1

Fractions and Proportional Reasoning: An Overview

Discussion of Activities

1. If 6 men can build a house in 3 days, then to shorten the time, you will need more men on the job. As the number of men goes up, the number of days goes down. Six men build $\frac{1}{3}$ of the house in one day, so 12 men could build $\frac{2}{3}$ of the house in one day, and 18 men could build $\frac{3}{3}$ of one whole house in a day (assuming that all of the men do an honest day's work). This means that it would take 3 times as many men to complete the job in $\frac{1}{3}$ the time.

2. If 6 chocolates cost $.93, then 12 would cost $1.86 and 24 would cost $3.72. If 6 cost $.93, then 2 cost $.31. The cost of 22 candies is $.31 less than $3.72 or $3.41.

3. John has 3 times as many marbles as Mark, so you can think of the whole set of marbles as 4 equal groups, with 3 of the groups in front of John and 1 group in front of Mark. If there are 32 marbles, each group contains 8 marbles. John has 24 marbles and Mark has 8 marbles.

4. If Mac does twice as much as his brother, he will do $\frac{2}{3}$ of the lawn, while his brother does $\frac{1}{3}$. If it takes Mac 45 minutes to do $\frac{3}{3}$ of the job, then it takes 15 minutes to do $\frac{1}{3}$ and 30 minutes to do $\frac{2}{3}$. Meanwhile, during that 30 minutes, his little brother does the other $\frac{1}{3}$ of the lawn.

5. The more people you have working, the faster the job will get done (assuming, of course, that the boys do not goof off on the job). If 6 boys were given 20 minutes to clean up, then 1 boy should be given 6 times as much time or 120 minutes. Then 9 would each require $\frac{1}{9}$ of the time needed by 1 person: $\frac{120}{9}$ or $\frac{40}{3}$ or $13\frac{1}{3}$ minutes. An-other way. If 6 boys can do the job in 20 minutes, then 3 would take 40 minutes. If

there are 9 people working, then each set of 3 people does $\frac{1}{3}$ of the job in 40 minutes, so the total time needed is $\frac{40}{3}$ minutes.

6. No answer. Knowing the weight of one player is not help in determining the weight of 11 players. People's weights are not related to each other.

7. Every time they put away $7, Sandra pays $2 and her mom pays $5. To get $210, they will need to make their respective contributions 30 times. In all, Sandra will contribute $60 and her mom will contribute $150.

8. If you decrease the number of people doing a job, it will take longer to finish the job. If you have $\frac{1}{3}$ the number of people working, they can get only $\frac{1}{3}$ as much done in the 96 minutes. Each $\frac{1}{3}$ of the job will take them 96 minutes, so they can do $\frac{2}{3}$ of work in 192 minutes and $\frac{3}{3}$ of the job (the whole job) in 288 minutes (4 hours and 48 minutes).

9. Reason down then reason up. The bike can run for 5 minutes on $.65 worth of fuel, and for 1 minute on $.13 worth of fuel. It can run for 6 minutes on $.78 worth of fuel and for 7 minutes on $.91 worth of fuel.

10. 15 to 1 = 150 to 10. Therefore, decreasing the number of faculty by 8 will give the required ratio.

11. Your shadow (8′) is 1.6 times as tall as you are (5′), so the shadow cast by the telephone pole must be 1.6 times as tall as the pole. If the shadow is 48′ and that is 1.6 times the real height of the telephone pole, the pole must be 30′ tall. Also, the telephone pole's shadow is 6 times as long as yours, so it must be 6 times as tall as you are.

12. In a square, two adjacent sides have the same length. That means that the ratio of the measure of one side to the measure of the other side would be 1. The rectangle that is most square is the one whose ratio of width to length is closest to 1. For the 35″ × 39″ rectangle, the ratio is $\frac{35}{39}$ or about .90; for the 22″ × 25″ rectangle, the ratio is $\frac{22}{25}$ or .88. This means that the 35″ × 39″ rectangle is most square.

13. Gear A has 1.5 times the number of teeth on gear B. So every time A turns once, B turns 1.5 times. If A makes 5.5 revolutions, B makes 5.5(1.5) or 8.25 revolutions.

14. The density or crowdedness of a town with cars is given by comparing the number of cars to the number of square miles in the town. For town A, the crowdedness is $\frac{12555}{15}$ $= 837 \frac{\text{cars}}{\text{sq mi}}$. For town B, it is $\frac{2502}{3} = 834 \frac{\text{cars}}{\text{sq mi}}$. For town C, it is $\frac{14212}{17} = 836 \frac{\text{cars}}{\text{sq mi}}$. The town least crowded with cars is town B. B must be Birmingham.

15. Several different approaches are given:

  a. In pitcher A, 4 out of 7 total cubes are cranberry; in B, 3 out of 5 total cubes are cranberry. Because $\frac{3}{5} > \frac{4}{7}$, B has a stronger cranberry taste.

  b. In pitcher A, the ratio of cranberry to apple is 4 to 3; in B, the ratio of cranberry to apple is 3 to 2. Because $\frac{3}{2} > \frac{4}{3}$, B has a stronger cranberry taste.

  c. In pitcher A, for each cube of cranberry, there is $\frac{3}{4}$ cube of apple. In pitcher B, for each cube of cranberry, there is $\frac{2}{3}$ cube of apple. Pitcher B has a stronger cranberry taste because for each unit of cranberry, there is less of the opposing flavor $\left(\frac{2}{3} < \frac{3}{4}\right)$.

  d. Imagine that the pitchers are very large. In pitcher A, make 3 batches, and in pitcher B, make 4 batches. In pitcher A, you would then have 12 cubes of cranberry and 9 cubes of apple, while in pitcher B, you would have 12 cranberry and only 8 apple. B would have the stronger cranberry taste because it has fewer cubes of apple for the same number of cranberry.

16. In a true enlargement, all dimensions grow by the same factor. Suppose the original picture measured 5 cm × 6.5 cm. If the picture were enlarged and the width increased from 5 to 9, it grew to 1.8 times its original width; the new length should also be 1.8 times the original length, or 11.7 cm. This means that the 9 cm × 10 cm picture is not its enlargement. Check each pair of pictures to find the cases where the length and width were both multiplied by the same factor in going from the smaller to the larger picture. You will find that picture B is an enlargement of picture C. Both dimensions of C are multiplied by 1.25.

17. There are several different ways in which this task could be accomplished. Here are four possibilities:

  • All 6 cats are needed to kill a rat. They polish him off in one minute, while the other rats stand by and wait their turn.
  • Three cats are needed to kill a rat, and they do it in 2 minutes.
  • Two cats kill a single rat, and they do it in 3 minutes.
  • Each cat kills a rat single-handedly and takes 6 minutes to do it.

  If you assume that the rats are dumb enough to stand by and wait their turn, that there is some orderly way of assigning the rats to each of the cats, and agree to disregard the foolishness of fractional cats and rats, here are some solutions:

  (i) If 6 cats together kill 1 rat in 1 minute, then it would take 12 cats to kill 2 rats in 1 minute. So if the 12 have 50 times as long to do it, they can kill 50 times as many rats (100 rats).

  (ii) If 3 cats kill 1 rat in 2 minutes, then 12 cats (4 times as many cats) could kill 4 rats (4 times as many rats) in 2 minutes. The same 12 cats could kill 25 times as many rats if they have 25 times as long to do it. So they could kill 100 rats in 50 minutes.

(iii) 6 cats / 1 rat / 1 minute
     6 cats / 300 rats / 300 minutes
     2 cats / 100 rats / 300 minutes
     12 cats / 100 rats / 50 minutes

18. When weights are placed farther from the fulcrum, they will exert a greater effect or downward pull. Weights closer to the fulcrum have a lesser effect. A heavier weight closer to the center may be counteracted by a smaller weight placed farther out. How much "tipping" you get depends on the weight you have put on each side and how far along the arm each weight is placed. In A, there are 3 weights on the left side, each 3 units from the fulcrum or $3(3) = 9$ units of pull. On the right side, there are 2 weights, each 4 units from the fulcrum or $2(4) = 8$ units of pull. The balance will tip to the left. In B, you have $1(4) + 2(3) + 1(2) = 12$ units of pull on the left, and $1(4) + 2(2) + 1(1) = 9$ units of pull on the right. Again, the beam will tip to the left. Also notice that in B, the far weights balance, while the closer weights are farther to the left.

19. A picture may be the best way to represent this situation. Shade $\frac{2}{3}$ of a rectangle to represent the married men and $\frac{3}{4}$ of another rectangle to represent the married women. Because the corresponding numbers of men and women are equal, position the rectangles so that the shaded parts overlap.

Then you can clearly see that the total number of women is the same as $\frac{8}{9}$ of the total number of men. The ratio of men to women is 9:8.

20. Let A be the coffee sold for $8 per pound, and B, the coffee sold for $14 per pound. If we buy A alone, we pay $8 per pound. If equal amounts of each type of coffee are used in the mixture (25 lb. of A and 25 lb. of B), then we will pay $11 per pound. There must be more of A because the mixture is selling for $10 per pound.

price per pound

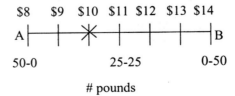

pounds

Because the cost of the mixture is $\frac{2}{3}$ of the way between \$8 and \$11, the amount of A must be $\frac{1}{3}$ of the way between 25 and 50 pounds. There are $33\frac{1}{3}$ pounds of coffee A, and the rest of the mixture ($16\frac{2}{3}$ pounds) must be coffee B.

ACTIVITIES

1. Using Mr. Short's measurements, we can see that 2 buttons are as tall as 3 paperclips. If Mr. Tall measures 6 buttons, that would be the same as 9 paperclips.

2. If 2 buttons are as tall as 3 paperclips, then five times as many buttons are as tall as 5 times as many paper clips. This means that 10 buttons have the same height as 15 paperclips. The length of Mr. Tall's car is 10 buttons. If 2 buttons are as tall as 3 paperclips, then 1 button is as tall as $1\frac{1}{2}$ paperclips. $7\frac{1}{2}$ paperclips are as wide as 2 + 2 + 1 = 5 buttons.

3. Jim paid \$2.13 per pound for his candy and Ann paid \$2.62 per pound for the same candy. Jim got the better deal.

Supplementary Activities

1. If we measure Mr. Peterson's height in basketballs, he is 6 balls tall. He is also as tall as a pile of 15 boxes. His son, Matt, is as tall as 4 basketballs. How many boxes will be as tall as Matt?

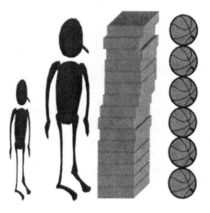

2. These aliens always carry an ample food supply. Alien #1 eats 3 food pellets per meal. Alien #2 eats 2 food pellets per meal. Which one has the most provisions?

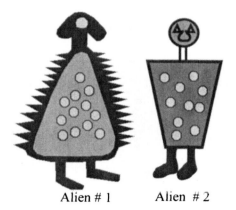

Alien # 1   Alien # 2

3. Do you get a better deal if you buy the magazine for a longer period of time?

Tremendous savings! 66% off the cover price!

College Life Magazine

Term	6 mos.	9 mos.	12 mos.
Your Price	8.00	12.00	16.50

Name _____

Address _____

City, State, Zip _____

Order NOW! We will bill you later!

4. I found this poster on a bulletin board. See if you can interpret it. Explain your findings.

NUMBER OF APPLICANTS PER COMMON
TEACHING POSITIONS

ELEMENTARY EDUCATION:
150 - 700 applicants for one position

PHYSICAL EDUCATION:
150 - 700 applicants for one position

SOCIAL SCIENCE:
150 - 700 applicants for one position

ENGLISH:
30 - 70 applicants for one position

MATH:
25 - 30 applicants for one position

SCIENCE:
25 - 30 applicants for one position

MUSIC / ART:
10 - 30 applicants for one position
(DEPENDING ON LOCATION)

**SPECIAL EDUCATION:
5 applicants for one position

2

Fractions and Rational Numbers

Discussion of Activities

1. One example is a combination problem: Joe's ice cream store sells three different flavors of ice cream, a choice or large or small cone or dish, and four different toppings. How many different purchases can you make at Joe's? A second example is an area problem: A rectangle is 5 cm. long and 3 cm. wide. What is its area? Another common type is a multiplicative comparison problem: Last month, Jack collected money from 135 customers on his paper route. This month, he collected from $\frac{3}{5}$ as many as last month. How many customers paid their bills this month?

2. A common example is a speed problem: If Mrs. Jones traveled 145 miles in $2\frac{1}{2}$ hours, what was her average speed for the trip? When you divide miles by hours, you get miles per hour.

3. Here is an example: For a project he is doing, Mr. Carter needs 15 pieces of rope each $\frac{3}{8}$ of a meter long. He has 5 meters of rope in the garage. How many pieces can he cut from the rope he has before he needs to buy more?

4. Here is one example: If a yard of materials costs $3.95, how much will $\frac{3}{8}$ of a yard cost?

5. Although you see three different models, a set model, an area model, and a number line model, all three figures represent the same relative amount, $\frac{2}{3}$. In each case, 2 out of 3 equal parts are shown.

6. a.   b.   c.

7. To write an average speed for a trip, you compare how much distance has been traveled to the time it took to travel, that is, you divide total distance by total time. You can then re-write your division (fraction) to obtain the number of miles per 1 hour.

a. $\dfrac{4 \text{ mi}}{15 \text{ min}} = \dfrac{16 \text{ mi}}{1 \text{ hr}}$. (4 miles per 15 minutes is the same rate as 16 miles per 1 hour.)

b. 3.75 minutes per 1 mile $= \dfrac{3.75 \text{ min}}{1 \text{ mile}}$ and this is the same relationship as $\dfrac{1 \text{ mi}}{3.75 \text{ min}}$.

Now express $\dfrac{1 \text{ mi}}{3.75 \text{ min}}$ in miles per hour: $\dfrac{16 \text{ mi}}{1 \text{ hr}}$.

c. $\dfrac{220 \text{ mi}}{4 \text{ hr}} = \dfrac{55 \text{ mi}}{1 \text{ hr}}$.

Supplementary Activities

1. In each example below, you are shown 2 pans of pizza. Ted gets the pizza in the first pan and Mindy gets the pizza in the second pan. Who gets more pizza? Justify your answer. Which characteristics were important and which were unimportant in comparing the amounts of pizza each person received?

   a.

   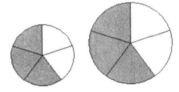

   b.

   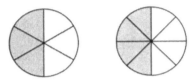

   c.

   d.

   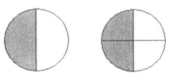

2. Solve this problem in your head. (Set up a "per" quantity.) $\frac{1}{2}$ liter of juice costs $1.89. At the same rate, what is the price per liter?

3. Solve this problem in your head. (Set up a "per" quantity.) John took one step and it measured .75 meters long. Would it take more than 10 or fewer than 10 steps to measure a distance of 10 meters?

4. If you eat $\frac{2}{3}$ of a 2-pack of granola bars will you eat the same amount as eating $\frac{1}{2}$ of a granola bar? Draw pictures and explain.

5. Figure out a way to tell (by looking, not by computing!) which multiplications will result in a product larger than $\frac{2}{3}$, and which will result in a product smaller than $\frac{2}{3}$.

a. $\dfrac{2}{3} \cdot \dfrac{2}{3}$ b. $\dfrac{2}{3} \cdot \dfrac{3}{2}$ c. $\dfrac{2}{3} \cdot \dfrac{3}{5}$ d. $\dfrac{2}{3} \cdot \dfrac{7}{8}$ e. $\dfrac{2}{3} \cdot \dfrac{3}{4}$ f. $\dfrac{2}{3} \cdot \dfrac{5}{3}$

6. In the rational numbers, multiplication distributes over addition. To multiply $3\dfrac{1}{2} \cdot 2\dfrac{1}{2}$,

first think of $3\dfrac{1}{2}$ as $3 + \dfrac{1}{2}$ and think of $2\dfrac{1}{2}$ as $2 + \dfrac{1}{2}$.

Think: $\left(2 + \dfrac{1}{2}\right)\left(3 + \dfrac{1}{2}\right)$ $(2 \cdot 3) = 6$

$\left(2 \cdot \dfrac{1}{2}\right) = 1$ So far I have 7.

Then $\left(2 + \dfrac{1}{2}\right)\left(3 + \dfrac{1}{2}\right)$ half of 3 is $1\dfrac{1}{2}$; now I have $8\dfrac{1}{2}$

half of a half is $\dfrac{1}{4}$; now I have $8\dfrac{3}{4}$.

Use this technique to do the following multiplications in your head.

a. $1\dfrac{1}{2} \cdot 3\dfrac{1}{2}$ b. $2\dfrac{1}{4} \cdot 4$ c. $3 \cdot 2\dfrac{1}{8}$ d. $2\dfrac{2}{3} \cdot 6\dfrac{1}{2}$

3

Relative and Absolute Thinking

Discussion of Activities

1. Both the King family and the Jones family have two girls. However, the families have different numbers of children, so that if we think about the number of girls as compared to (or relative to) the number of boys or to the total number of children, then the situation looks different in each family. In the Jones family, $\frac{2}{5}$ of the children are girls and in the King family, $\frac{2}{4}$ or $\frac{1}{2}$ of the children are girls. The ratio of girls to boys in the Jones family is 2:3, while in the King family, it is 2:2. Therefore, the King family has a greater proportion of girls.

2. Merely by counting the brown eggs in each container, we can tell that the 18-egg container has more brown eggs. However, we might consider the fact that the containers hold different numbers of eggs. 7 out of the 18 eggs or $\frac{7}{18}$ are brown. Six out of the 12 eggs or $\frac{6}{12}$ or $\frac{1}{2}$ of the dozen are brown. Seven is less than half of 18, so a greater portion of the dozen eggs is brown.

3. Yes, Bert is correct.

4. The answer to "how much" is not a number of slices. Pan B contains $\frac{3}{8}$ of a pizza more than pan A contains. You could serve up the amount of pizza in pan A $2\frac{1}{2}$ times from the pizza in B. Note that these comparisons are OK in this situation because the pizzas are the same size. If they were not, these questions would not be meaningful.

5. You can tell who walked farther merely by adding the distances that each person walked. Dan walked 6 miles and Tasha walked 7 miles. To decide who walked faster, you need to compare distance to the time it took to walk it. Dan traveled his 6 miles in 2.5 hours, so his speed was $\frac{6 \text{ mi}}{2.5 \text{ hr}} = 2.4 \frac{\text{mi}}{\text{hr}}$. Tasha walked her 7 miles in the same amount of time, so her speed was $\frac{7 \text{ mi}}{2.5 \text{ hr}} = 2.8 \frac{\text{mi}}{\text{hr}}$. Tasha walked faster.

6. Five out of the dozen eggs are colored and 6 out of the 18-pack are colored. $\frac{6}{18} = \frac{1}{3}$ but $\frac{1}{3}$ of 12 is 4. Therefore the dozen has more brown eggs.

7. If is more helpful to know the percent of discount because then you know the amount you can save on an item of any price. 20% mean that you will save $.20 for every dollar that you spend. If someone tells you only a dollar amount, you cannot tell if it is a good sale or not. $2.00 off on an item whose original cost was $500 is hardly worth the effort of rushing down to the store, but a savings of $2.00 on a $5.00 item is a substantial savings (40%).

8. To judge the crowdedness of an elevator, you need to know how many people are on the elevator; however, that is not enough information. You might not call it crowded if there are ten people on an elevator that holds 25 people, but if there are 10 people on an elevator that holds 8, things are tighter! The number of people on the elevator must be compared to the recommended capacity or to the floor area (the number of square feet of floor space) in order to be able to tell if the elevator is crowded or not. If both elevators have the same capacity, the choice is clearly A, but if they do not have the same capacity, relative thinking is needed.

9. At table A, for each root beer served, $1\frac{1}{2}$ colas were served. At table B, for each root beer served, $1\frac{1}{3}$ colas were served. You can think of it this way: At table B, the root beer is not as diluted by cola as the root beer at Table A, so the people at table B consumed more root beer.

10. Leesa is correct.

11. Some possibilities are:
   a. What part of the pack did the girls chew? What part of the pack did they save for later? Is a greater portion of the package chewed or saved for later?
   b. What part of the 6-pack was given to the food pantry? What part of the pack did the people drink?

Supplementary Activities

1.

How many more stars are there in box B than in box A?

How many times the number of stars in A are in B?

Set A is what part of set B?

If there are two stars in a group, how many groups did it take to make Box A? Box B?

2. Can you tell by looking at the following pools which one has a greater capacity? Which pool has the greater area? In addition to the area, what quantity is needed to describe capacity? By choosing appropriate depth for each of the pools, show that sometimes the first pool might have the greater capacity, and sometimes the second might have the greater capacity.

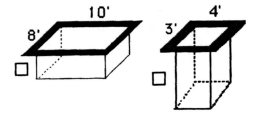

3. Today there is a sale at Neville's Women's Shop: $10.00 off the sticker price of every item! Describe exactly how you can tell which is a better buy, a dress marked $44.99 or a blouse marked $26.99.

4. What does it mean to say that a grasshopper can jump relatively higher than a person can?

5. The Manhattan Mercury reported that in 1950, when there was a population of 19,000 people, there were 12 people per acre in the city of Manhattan, Kansas. By 1995, when the population was 43,000, there were only 5 people per acre. Interpret this information as completely as possible.

6. There were 7 males and 12 females in the Dew Drop Inn on Monday night. In the Game Room next door, there were 14 males and 24 females. Which spot had more females?

7. The first picture shows Jeb and Sarah Smart when they were younger. The second shows them as they look now. Who grew faster between the first and second pictures?

8. A car was traveling at a speed of 65 mph and a truck was traveling on the same road at a speed of 60 mph. They came to a hill and both vehicles slowed down by 15 mph as they climbed the hill. Which vehicle had a harder time maintaining its speed?

9. Adam, a fifth grader was asked the following question about growing trees. Analyze his response.

   A tree that was 8 feet high last year is 14 feet high this year. Another tree that was 10 feet high last year is also 14 feet high this year. Which tree grew faster?

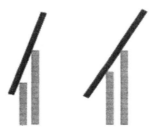

   Adam used unifix cubes to build models of the trees, showing last year's heights and this year's heights. He placed a ruler on top of both models of tree A and another ruler on top of both models of tree B. "The ruler that goes up the most tells me the one that grew faster," he explained.

10. The class with the most monthly attendance awards for the year gets a pizza party! Mr. Jones, the principal asked you to make arrangements for the party. You found out that the third grade and fourth grade classes had the most awards. You collected the following data from the teachers in those classes, and now you must choose only one class for the pizza party. Describe several different perspectives that could be used to make the decision.

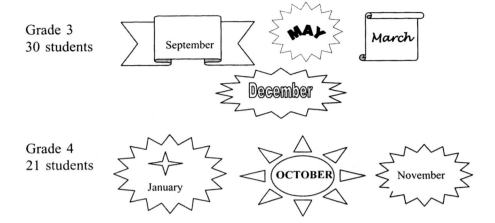

Grade 3
30 students

Grade 4
21 students

11. Athlete's Shoes has Flyers and Moonwalkers on sale. Last week they sold 100 pairs of Flyers and 15 pairs of Moonwalkers. They week, they sold 200 pairs of Flyers and 45 pairs of Moonwalkers. Which kind of shoes had the best *increase* in sales this week as compared to last week? Explain.

12. In each case, describe A in terms of the quantity B, then describe B in terms of the quantity A, using multiplicative comparisons.

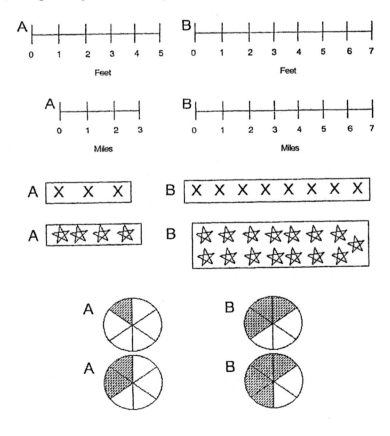

4

Measurement

Discussion of Activities

1. How sour a mixture is depends not only on the amount of vinegar, but on the amount of vinegar as compared to the amount of sugar. We might compare the number of teaspoons of vinegar to the number of teaspoons of sugar: $\dfrac{\text{\# teaspoons of vinegar}}{\text{\# teaspoons of sugar}}$. Using this ratio, the higher number would indicate the more sour taste. For bowl A, $\dfrac{8}{10} = .8$ and for bowl B, $\dfrac{6}{8} = .75$.

2. What does it mean to be square? In a square, two adjacent sides have the same length, so if you compared them, you would get a ratio of 1:1. Find the ratios of adjacent sides in each of the rectangles and see how close they are to 1. The ratio of adjacent sides for the 114′ × 99′ rectangle is $\dfrac{99}{114}$ or .87. The ratio of adjacent sides for the 455′ × 494′ rectangle is $\dfrac{455}{494}$ or .92. The ratio for the 284′ × 265′ rectangle is $\dfrac{265}{284}$ or .93. The 284′ × 265′ rectangle is most square.

3. Ty doesn't understand that inverse relationship between the number of parts and the size of the parts. You might get him to think about it by asking, "Your Mom has 2 identical cherry pies. She cuts one into 9 equal pieces and the other into 5 equal pieces. You really like her cherry pie. From which pie do you want to have your piece?"

4. Fred does not understand the compensatory principle of measurement. The size of the pizza (its area) isn't going to change. If you cut it into more slices, each slice will be smaller; if you cut it into fewer slices, each slice will be larger.

5. The oranginess of the drinks depends on the amount of orange as compared to the amount of water. For pitcher A, $\dfrac{\text{\# cans o.j.}}{\text{\# cans H}_2\text{O}} = \dfrac{2}{2} = 1$. For pitcher B, $\dfrac{\text{\# cans o.j.}}{\text{\# cans H}_2\text{O}} = \dfrac{3}{4} = .75$. The larger the ratio, the more orangey the mixture will taste. So the juice in pitcher A will taste more orangey.

6. The blackness of the ink depends on the amount of amount of water added. Both companies use a recipe in which the water added is half as much as the amount of black

dye, so we would expect both ink mixtures to look equally black. To measure black-ness of the ink, we need to compare the amount of black dye to the amount of water. For the India Ink company, $\dfrac{\text{\# parts black dye}}{\text{\# parts H}_2\text{O}} = \dfrac{3}{1.5} = 2$. For the Midnight Ink Com-

pany, $\dfrac{\text{\# parts black dye}}{\text{\# parts H}_2\text{O}} = \dfrac{2}{1} = 2$. Our measure confirms our expectations.

7. Assuming you like cookies, *better* means that if you joined the group, you would get more cookies. To judge which group would be better for you, you would want to see if the number of cookies as compared to the number of people in the group is greater. If you joined Tom's group, there would be 8 cookies for 5 people, or $\dfrac{8}{5} = 1.6$ cookies for each person. If you joined Jenny's group, there would be 11 cookies for 6 people, or $\dfrac{11}{6}$ = 1.8 cookies per person. It is going to be difficult to divide the cookies in either case, but assuming that it could be done, you would get slightly more cookie in Jenny's group.

8. To decide which ramp is steeper, you cannot merely measure the height up to the door. The steepness of a ramp is going to depend on the horizontal distance over which that rise occurs. If it occurs in a very short distance, the ramp will be steep; if it occurs over a long distance, the ramp will not be too steep. If you made the ramp to the doorway that is 5′ high the same length as the one to the 2′ high doorway, then the ramp to the 5′ high doorway would be very steep. However, if you started that ramp farther away from the building, you could decrease its steepness. By starting sufficiently far away from the building, you could give it the same steepness as the ramp to the 2′ high door.

9. We might measure how hungry each character was by comparing how many food pel-lets he ate to the number he usually eats. For Spotsy, that would be $\dfrac{6}{4} = 1.5$, meaning that he ate 1.5 the amount he usually eats. For Dynamo, we get $\dfrac{9}{6} = 1.5$, meaning that he also ate 1.5 times the amount he usually eats. So they were equally hungry.

10. All three countries are not the same size, so we cannot simply look at the population figures. We need more information. For example, we might compare each population to the area of its respective country in square miles.

11. a. $7\dfrac{3}{4}$ inches   b. $4\dfrac{1}{4}$ inches

12. a. 10 inches   b. 10 inches   c. $9\dfrac{3}{4}$ inches   d. $9\dfrac{5}{8}$ inches

13. a. $5\dfrac{1}{2}$ units

b. Divide the strip into 3 equal lengths and place 2 of them end-to-end.

c. (any two parts out of the three) but not .

Whether you are partitioning a unit of length or a unit of area, you must be sure that you make pieces of equal length or of equal area. If you partition the triangle using horizontal lines, you cannot be sure that your pieces are of equal area.

Supplementary Activities

1. Which juice will taste more orangey, the juice in pitcher A, or the juice in pitcher B?

Pitcher A   Pitcher B

3 cans o.j.   4 cans o.j.
2 cans H_2O 1 can H_2O

2. Below you see the end of a strip whose left endpoint is placed at 0 on the ruler.
   a. What is its length to the nearest inch?
   b. To the nearest half inch?
   c. To the nearest quarter inch?
   d. What is its length to the nearest sixteenth of an inch?

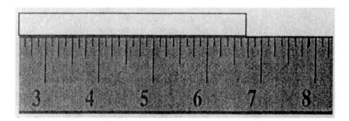

3. Below you see the end of a strip whose left endpoint is placed at 0 on the ruler.
   a. What is its length to the nearest inch?
   b. To the nearest half inch?
   c. To the nearest quarter inch?
   d. What is its length to the nearest sixteenth of an inch?

4. Which property is more square?
   Property A: 60' × 90'   Property B: 75' × 110'

5. Here is Sen's response to question 4. Is he correct?

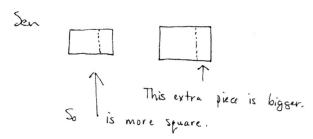

6. How steep is this ramp?

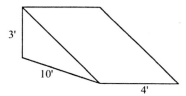

7. Here is Mark's response to problem 6. Is he correct?

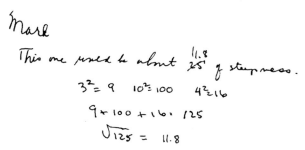

8. Sam and Jason, two third graders, commented on the following pictures:

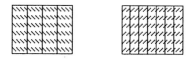

Sam said that $\frac{7}{7}$ is larger because there are more pieces. Jason said that $\frac{4}{4}$ is larger because the pieces are bigger. How would you explain this situation? What principle do you suspect that the boys do not understand?

9. Sure Foot ran 12 furlongs in 22 seconds. High Stepper ran 6 furlongs in 1 minute 10 seconds. Which horse ran faster? How do you measure fastness?

10. Below you see the end of a strip whose left endpoint is placed at 0 on the ruler.
   a. What is its length to the nearest inch?
   b. To the nearest half inch?

c. To the nearest quarter inch?

d. What is its length to the nearest sixteenth of an inch?

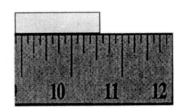

11.

Sam the shark eats 7 small fish every 3 hours. Which of the following sharks have a bigger appetite than Sam does. How do you measure a bigger appetite?

	Eats this many fish	Every
Sylvester	5	2 hours
Snort	9	4 hours
Spike	15	8 hours
Spiffy	11	6 hours
Stanley	13	5 hours

12. Which would be steeper, a stretch of highway with a 10% grade or this ramp?

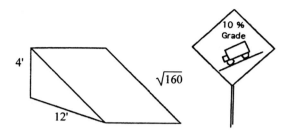

13. Which of these figures is more round? How do you measure roundness?

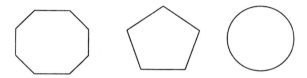

14. The Chicago Bulls and the Detroit Pistons once played each another in January and in March of the same season. The games brought two great stars into the same court. In January, Michael Jordan scored 30 points and Isaiah Thomas scored 20 points. In March, Jordan scored 40 points and Thomas scored 30 points. The following bar graph shows this information. Explain which player's performance improved the most.

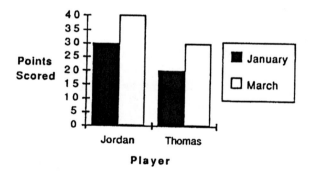

15. How can you tell which ski ramp is steeper?

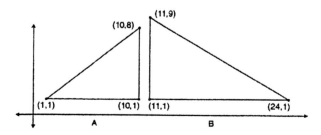

5

Quantities and Covariation

Discussion of Activities

1. In a caricature, the artist deliberately draws some feature(s) out of proportion to the rest of the face or body. Sometimes, the intention may be to emphasize a particular characteristic of the person. For example, in the caricature of Mark Twain, the artist may have been trying to capture something of his character. His long, white hair and mustache give him a kindly, grandfatherly appearance. His ear is way out of proportion with the rest of his head, perhaps suggesting that he would be a good listener, like a grandfather to whom you could go when you had a problem. Sometimes the artist is trying to reflect personal or popular sentiment about a person. This is usually the case in the caricature of a political figure. In the second picture, the artist depicts Prince Charles with a head out of proportion to the rest of his body. Charles' ears, which normally stand out from his head, are drawn out of proportion to the rest of his head, thus giving him a "Dumbo" look. This caricature gives a double message. The artists sees Charles as a person who thinks highly of himself, and at the same time is rather stupid-looking in the eyes of the public.

2. The pizza was not distributed fairly among the three groups. The 45 students received a smaller portion of the pizza than the 45 parents and teachers received, and the parents received a larger portion than the teachers. The portions were not proportional to the numbers of people who ate from them.

3. As always, answers are not necessarily unique.

picture:frame :: yard:fence	R : in enclosed by
giraffe:neck :: porcupine:quills	R : is best known for
food:body :: rain:earth	R : nourishes
car:gasoline :: sail:wind	R : is fueled by
sap:tree :: blood:body	R : flows through
sandwich:boy :: carrot:rabbit	R : is food for
pear:tree :: potato:ground	R : is grown in
tree:leaves :: book:pages	R : is composed of
conductor:train :: captain:ship	R : is the commander of
wedding:bride :: funeral:corpse	R : is a ceremony for

4. 1) 1 to 1

   2) 1 to 4

   3) 1 to 2

   4) 1 to 3

5. a. No. Orange is twice the length of yellow, but green is more than twice the length of white.

   b. No. Green is 3 times the length of white, but dark green is only twice the length of green.

   c. No. Green is half the length of dark green, but purple is less than half the length of blue.

   d. Yes. Purple is half of brown and yellow is half of orange.

   e. No. Blue is 3 times as long as green, but red is only twice as long as white.

6. Of course, the answer depends on the height of the person answering the question. Assume that the height of the dog is roughly $\frac{1}{4}$ the height of the person (using knee, waist, chest, top of head as quarter marks). Also assume that the person answering the question is about 5 feet tall. That means the dog would be about $1\frac{1}{4}$ feet high. Then if we increase proportionately, the person grows to $1\frac{3}{5}$ of his or her height. The dog must do the same. This would make the dog about 2 feet high.

7. a. 2 orange

   b. orange + purple

   c. purple

   d. red

   e. black

8. a. Dianne was faster today.

   b. She was slower today.

   c. She was faster today.

   d. She was faster today.

   e. We can not draw any conclusions if Dianne ran fewer laps in less time than she did yesterday.

9. a. Changing quantities include the amount of gas in your tank, the number of gallons registered on the gas pump, the price registered on the gas pump, and time.

   b. Changing quantities include time, distance from your starting point, amount of gas in your tank, and your speed.

c. Changing quantities include shopping time, the amount of each purchase, and your total spent.

d. Changing quantities include time since you started, your depth, pressure, amount of air in your tank, and the amount of sunlight reaching you.

e. Changing quantities include time, depth of the water in the tub, and volume of water in the tub.

10. a. The amount of money put into the machine changed; time changed; the ratio (2 dimes + 1 nickel):1 quarter did not change.

b. The size of the flower changed, but the shape of the flower did not change.

c. The real distances between the cities do not change; the distance between any two cities on the map does not change; the ratio of 1 inch on the map to 20 miles in reality does not change.

d. The length of the room does not change; the unit of measure changes; the relationship between inches and feet does not change (12" = 1 ft).

e. The number of pies changes; the cost of each package changes; the cost per pie (or the cost per 7 pies) does not change.

11. a. There are more peas than carrots.

b. Ted is taller.

c. More people have cats.

d. It will cost less than $3.

e. More fathers than mothers came to school; some students had both parents present.

12. a. ↓↑ 8 hours

Here is a way to think about this situation: The 8 people each work for 2 hours; that gives a total of 16 hours of work. If 2 people share the work, they will work together for 8 hours.

b. ↓↓ $6

c. ↑↑ 12 hours

d. People's ages do not work that way. Every son does not have a mother 3 times as old as he is.

e. ↓↑ 6 hours. Think about this situation the same way we did about part a.

f. The percentage charged for sales tax stays fixed no matter what size purchase you make.

g. Increasing the number of people does not increase the amount of time for the meal.

h. ↑↓ 10 minutes

Supplementary Activities

1. $\frac{1}{3}$ of a pound of cheese costs $2.50. Will $\frac{4}{3}$ as much coast more than $2.50 or less than $2.50?

2. There are 6 times as many dogs as cats at our SPCA. Are there more dogs or more cats?

3. Troy runs $\frac{4}{3}$ as fast as Mike. Who will win a foot race, Troy or Mike?

4. Elena's team can do a job in $\frac{2}{3}$ the time that Manny's team can do the same job. What can you say about this situation?

5. In a certain village, $\frac{2}{3}$ of the men are married to $\frac{3}{4}$ of the women. Are there more men or more women in the village?

6. Decide whether the following statements make sense or not. If the statement is correct, write "C." If a statement does not make sense, fix it by changing one of the numbers in the statement. If you cannot fix it, say why.

   a. If an orchestra can play a symphony in 1 hour, then if 2 orchestras play together, they can probably play it in $\frac{1}{2}$ hour.

   b. If it takes 3 brothers 15 minutes to drive to the soccer field to see a game, then 1 brother could drive to the game by himself in 5 minutes.

   c. If 1 boy has 3 sisters, then 2 boys probably have 6 sisters.

   d. If it takes 3 boys 2 hours to deliver papers on a certain route, then 6 boys could probably do the route in 1 hour.

   e. If a girl can walk to the mall in 20 minutes, then when she walks with 2 of her friends, they can probably get there in 60 minutes.

7. If you arms were 6 feet long, how tall would you be?
   With a colleague or partner, discuss (a) the relationships that might be important for solving the problem and (b) some of the vocabulary you need to talk about the problem. When Kevin, a sixth grader, thought about this problem, here is what he said. Analyze the following excerpt of Kevin's discussion to determine whether his answer is correct and in which directions his thinking needs to develop.

   I: If your arms were six feet long, how tall would you be?
   K: (Long pause.) Six feet one.
   I: Why do you say that?
   K: 'Cause you don't want your fingers to drag on the ground.

I: Show me with your thumb and your pointer finger how long an inch is.

K: (Shows a length of approximately two inches.)

I: Seems to me, if your fingers were only an inch off the ground, you would bump them on every stone you passed.

K: Yeah, I guess you would.

I: Well what do you think about that?

K: I guess you better have them up a few more inches. Probably five or six.

8. Discuss each of the quantities listed by the sixth graders discussing the tractor problem. Be sure to answer these questions: Does the quantity change? Is it related to any of the other quantities? If so, how?

- Distance between the wheels
- Distance each wheel travels
- How fast the wheels turn
- Time it takes each wheel to complete one turn
- The circumference of the wheels
- How many times each wheel turns
- Number of turns of the smaller wheel as compare to number of turns of the larger wheel

9. Complete each analogy and state the relationship that led you to your answer.
   a. fire : ashes :: special occasion : ?
   b. soccer : sport :: hammer : ?
   c. sun : day :: rise : ?
   d. train : freight :: ship : ?
   e. square : octagon :: triangle : ?
   f. graceful : clumsy :: late : ?
   g. presto : instantly :: unlike : ?
   h. string : yellow ribbon :: finger : ?
   i. thieves : den :: cards : ?
   j. body : helmet :: finger : ?

10. For each pair shown below, tell whether the second picture could be an enlargement of the first. Explain why or why not.

   a.

b.

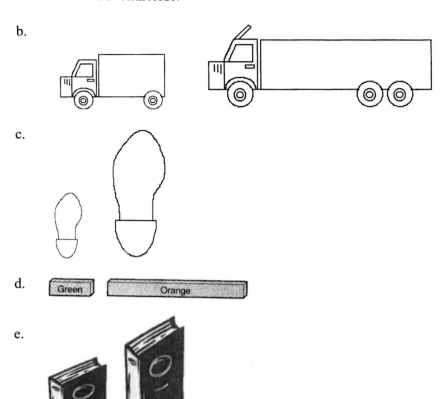

c.

d.

e.

11. If a train entered this tunnel, would it be able to get out the other end?

What quantities would you use in explaining this situation to children?

12. A four-year-old child drew this picture of a bird and flower in some grass on a sunny day. List everything about the picture that you would expect a third grader with a good visual sense of proportion to recognize about the drawing.

13. Imagine pouring the liquid in each glass into the glass on the right. Draw the level you would expect the liquid to reach and using appropriate language and relevant quantities, explain your drawing.

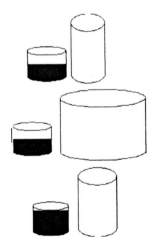

14. a. Suppose these wheels each make 3 full turns. Will both wheels cover the same distance? How do you know?

   b. Suppose both wheels travel a distance of 1 mile. Will they both make the same number of turns? How do you know?

15. Construct all 9 "yesterday and today" statements about each situation. Name the changing quantities and tell how they change.

   a. Yesterday I made juice by mixing some concentrate with some water.

   b. Yesterday I walked a certain distance in a certain amount of time.

16. Leonardo Da Vinci expressed the proportions of the human body in this drawing. Study the picture and tell as much as you can about body proportions.

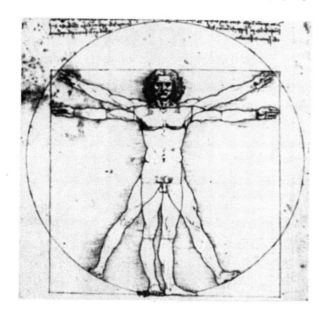

17. Here you can see some pottery. It takes 15 cups of water or 9 bottles of water to fill the jug. It also takes 10 cups of water to fill the pitcher. How many bottles of water does it take to fill the pitcher? Which quantities remain constant (invariant)?

jug   bottle   cup   pitcher

18. Here are two boxes, a 1″ cube and a 4″ cube.

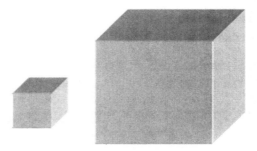

    a. How many of the smaller boxes would it take to fill the large one?

    b. Suppose I make the edge of the smaller box twice its present length. How many small boxes would fit inside the large one?

    c. Suppose I made the edge of the larger box twice its present length. How many of the small boxes would it hold?

    d. Suppose I double the lengths of the edges of both boxes. How many small boxes will fit inside the large box?

19. Now I have some blocks on a scale. This picture shows the scale in balance. These blocks may not be broken.

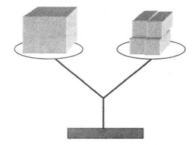

    a. What would happen if you replaced the block on the left with a block that is twice as heavy and you replaced each block on the right with one that is twice as heavy?

    b. If you replaced the block on the left with one that is $\frac{3}{4}$ as heavy, what would you have to do to the right side to balance the scale?

    c. If you replaced the blocks on the right with blocks that are $\frac{3}{4}$ as heavy, what would you have to do to the left side to balance the scale?

    d. If you replaced the large block with one that is $\frac{2}{3}$ its present weight, what would you have to do to the right side to balance the scale?

20. In Mrs. Brown's class, there are $\frac{5}{3}$ as many students are in Mrs. Henderson's class.

    a. Which teacher has more students?

    b. If you know the number of students in Mrs. Henderson's class, how do you find the number of students in Mrs. Brown's class?

    c. If you know the number of students in Mrs. Brown's class, how do you find the number of students in Mrs. Henderson's class?

    d. If Mrs. Henderson has 27 students, how many does Mrs. Brown have?

    e. If Mrs. Brown has 30 students, how many does Mrs. Henderson have?

6

Reasoning Up and Down

Discussion of Activities

1. All of these may constitute the unit in a fraction problem, depending, of course, on the context of the problem. The unit must be explicitly or implicitly designated or else you have ambiguity. Without context, you would not know, for example, whether part e shows a 3-unit (a unit consisting of 3 pieces) or 3 units.

2. a. 12 stars $= \frac{4}{3}$; 3 stars $= \frac{1}{3}$; 6 stars $= \frac{2}{3}$

   b. 6 balls $= \frac{3}{5}$; 2 balls $= \frac{1}{5}$; 10 balls $= \frac{5}{5} = 1$; 5 balls $= \frac{1}{2}$

   c. 12 sticks $= \frac{4}{3}$; 3 sticks $= \frac{1}{3}$; 9 sticks $= \frac{3}{3} = 1$; 5 sticks $= \frac{5}{9}$

   d. 8 blocks $= \frac{8}{3}$; 1 block $= \frac{1}{3}$; 3 blocks $= \frac{3}{3} = 1$; 6 blocks $= 2$

   e. 15 dots $= \frac{5}{6}$; 3 dots $= \frac{1}{6}$; 18 dots $= \frac{6}{6} = 1$; 9 dots $= \frac{1}{2}$; 27 dots $= 1\frac{1}{2}$

   f. 10 diamonds $= \frac{5}{4}$; 2 diamonds $= \frac{1}{4}$; 8 diamonds $= \frac{4}{4} = 1$; 3 diamonds $= \frac{3}{8}$

3. Both students are correct, and although they did not write down their reasoning process in the way we have done it in this chapter, each of them used a version of reasoning up and down. P went from $\frac{3}{8}$ to $\frac{1}{8}$, splitting up the 15 cards equally among the boxes in his picture. Then he extended the 5 cards per $\frac{1}{8}$ deck to all of the other boxes in order to get the number of cards in $\frac{8}{8}$. Rob used the same process, except that he went from $\frac{1}{8}$ to $\frac{2}{8}$ because he realized that he already knew how many cards were in $\frac{6}{8}$ of the deck and he only needed the number of cards in $\frac{2}{8}$ deck to complete the whole.

4. The fractions quoted by Frank and Dave refer to different units. Frank's statement used Dave's 15 pieces of pizza as the unit, while Dave used Frank's 12 pieces of pizza as the unit.

5. 11 small rectangles = $\frac{11}{3}$; 1 small rectangle = $\frac{1}{3}$; 3 small rectangles = $\frac{3}{3}$; 4 small rectangles = $\frac{4}{3}$ = $1\frac{1}{3}$.

6. The same unit should be used to represent each fraction in a side-by-side representation so that the sizes of the fractions relative to each other are accurately portrayed. Because the unit is different for each fraction, a child could draw some inappropriate conclusions (e.g., $\frac{1}{2}$ and $\frac{1}{5}$ are equivalent because the same number of equal parts are shaded for both and that $\frac{2}{3}$ and $\frac{2}{4}$ are equivalent because the same number of parts are shaded for both). In order to represent all of the fractions using the same unit, that unit would have to consist of 60 blocks. Color 30, 40, 30, and 12, for $\frac{1}{2}$, $\frac{2}{3}$, $\frac{2}{4}$, and $\frac{1}{5}$, respectively.

7. a. Partition the two circles in the unit into 3 equal pieces each. Then the shaded amount corresponds to $\frac{2}{6}$ or $\frac{1}{3}$ of the unit.

b. Partition the given circle into sixths; then the shaded amount is $\frac{4}{6}$. Compare with the given unit. It is $1\frac{1}{3}$.

c. If you partition each piece of the new unit into 3 pieces, then you can see that the shaded parts are 2 out of 12 or $\frac{1}{6}$.

8. a.  b. c.

d.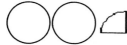

9. The critical idea in this problem is the unit. Each person received the same amount of cake, a portion that was equivalent to $\frac{1}{6}$ of the original cake. However, as each new person takes a piece, their fraction of the cake is based on a new unit, namely, the amount of cake that remains in the pan.

10. 8 spaces = $1\frac{1}{3}$ or $\frac{4}{3}$; 2 spaces = $\frac{1}{3}$; 6 spaces = 1. If 6 spaces = 1, then the subunits marked on the number line are each $\frac{1}{6}$ of the unit. The point X represents a length $\frac{5}{6}$ of the unit.

11. The three slices of turkey Ruth bought were $\frac{1}{3}$ of a pound. In order to determine how much $\frac{1}{4}$ pound is, you must first know what the unit is. If 3 slices = $\frac{1}{3}$ pound, then 9 slices = 1 pound. If 1 pound or $\frac{4}{4}$ = 9 slices, then $\frac{1}{4}$ pound must be $2\frac{1}{4}$ slices.

12. a. yellow = 3; b. blue = $\frac{2}{9}$; c. 1 = 2 yellows; d. yellow; e. green = $1\frac{1}{2}$, red = $4\frac{1}{2}$, and yellow = 9.

13. The first question we need to ask as we consider this problem is "What is the unit?" We should notice that a small pizza and a medium pizza were ordered, so that we cannot combine them and say there were 16 slices. Those 16 slices are different sizes! The unit is 8 small slices + 8 medium slices. How much was eaten? The only way to say it is $\frac{2}{8}$ or $\frac{1}{4}$ of the small pizza and $\frac{3}{8}$ of the medium pizza.

14. 16 liters = $\frac{2}{5}$; 8 liters = $\frac{1}{5}$; 40 liters = 1. The full tank holds 40 liters.

Supplementary Activities

1. Solve by reasoning up and down.

 $= \frac{3}{7}$

 = 1

$\triangle \triangle \triangle = \frac{1}{4}$

$= \frac{2}{3}$

$= \frac{1}{3}$

$= \frac{2}{9}$

$= \frac{2}{3}$

$= \frac{1}{2}$

$\begin{array}{c}\bigcirc\bigcirc\bigcirc\bigcirc\\\bigcirc\bigcirc\bigcirc\bigcirc\end{array} = \frac{2}{5}$

$= \frac{1}{10}$

2. Tell what fraction each x represents. Solve by reasoning up and down.

a.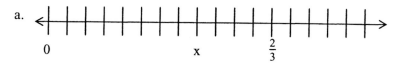

b.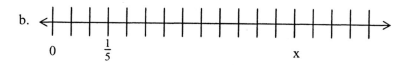

c.

0   x $\frac{9}{4}$

d.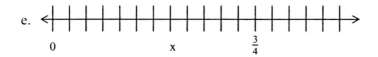

0                              $\frac{5}{6}$ x

e.

0   x $\frac{3}{4}$

f.

0                    $1\frac{1}{2}$ x

3. Find the missing component of each statement.

a. |——————————| is $\frac{5}{3}$ of

b.   is $\frac{1}{4}$ of □

c. 3 pounds is _____ of 4 ounces

d. 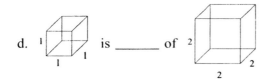 is _____ of

e. is $1\frac{2}{3}$ of _____

f. |————| is $\frac{2}{3}$ of

g. is _____ of

h. _____ is $\frac{2}{3}$ of ⬡

i. 350 cm is _____ of 42 dm

j.   is $\frac{5}{4}$ of ⊢——————⊣

k. is $\frac{1}{12}$ of

l.   is $\frac{1}{4}$ of

m. is _____ of 25 g

n. ☆☆ is $\frac{2}{7}$ of _____

o. 2 carats is _____ of $\frac{1}{3}$ carat

4. Use fraction blocks to complete this chart.

Green	Blue	Red	Yellow
1			
			3
		2	
			$\frac{2}{3}$
			$1\frac{1}{2}$
$\frac{1}{10}$			
		$\frac{3}{8}$	
		4	
	$\frac{1}{9}$		
		$\frac{2}{3}$	

5. Name the amount shaded in this picture in relation to each unit.

a. If the unit is ⬭⬭ the shaded amount represents _____ .

b. If the unit is ⌒ the shaded amount represents _____ .

c. If the unit is ◯◯◯ the shaded amount represents _____ .

d. If the unit is ⌒◯ the shaded amount represents _____ .

6. I have $\frac{5}{6}$ pie in my refrigerator. If I eat half a pie, how much will I have left? Analyze the work of the two students shown here.

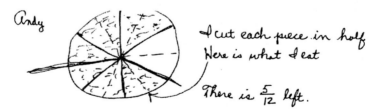

Andy

I cut each piece in half
Here is what I eat

There is $\frac{5}{12}$ left.

Barb

$\bigcirc - \bigcirc = \frac{2}{6}$ or $\frac{1}{3}$ left.

7. Tim spent $\frac{1}{4}$ of his money, and John spent half of his. How could it be possible that Tim spent more money than John spent?

8. Comment on this picture:

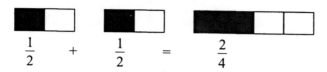

7

Unitizing

Discussion of Activities

1.

Every one of the whole pies is $3(\frac{1}{3}$-pies), so altogether the manager has 22 $(\frac{1}{3}$-pies) or $11(\frac{2}{3}$-pies).

2. a.    **b.**

c. 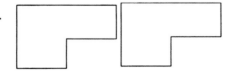   **d.**

e.

3. a. $5\frac{4}{6}$(6-packs)   **b.** $1\frac{10}{24}$(24-packs)   **c.** $1\frac{16}{18}$(18-packs)   **d.** $4\frac{2}{8}$(8-packs)

    e. $68(\frac{1}{2}$-cans)   **f.** $136(\frac{1}{4}$-cans)   **g.** 17(pairs)

4. a. Look at the rows in the picture.
    b. Look at the columns in the picture.
    c. Look at individual hearts.
    d. Look at pairs of hearts.

5. Some possibilities are:

a. 15 stars = 3(5-packs) = $7\frac{1}{2}$(pairs) = $1\frac{3}{12}$(dozen) = $30(\frac{1}{2}$-stars)

b. 16 colas = 8(pair) = $48(\frac{1}{3}$-cans) = $\frac{1}{2}$(32-pack)

c. 26 eggs = $2\frac{2}{12}$(dozen) = $52(\frac{1}{2}$-eggs) = $8\frac{2}{3}$(3-packs)

6. a. Look at the medium rectangle.

b. Look at the 9 small squares or the large square or the 4 medium squares.

c. Look at a set of 3 small squares.

d. Look at one of the small rectangles.

e. Look at a set of 2 medium squares.

7. a. $\frac{1}{4}$ b. $\frac{1}{18}$ c. $\frac{1}{3}$ d. $\frac{1}{8}$ e. $\frac{1}{54}$ f. $\frac{1}{24}$ g. $\frac{1}{16}$ h. $\frac{1}{6}$

Supplementary Activities

1. Four friends wanted a snack. Mrs. Johnson had 3 large cookies. Amy planned to split them this way:

   Seth planned to split them this way:

   a. Name the share that each of the friends get using Amy's plan.
   b. Name the share that each person gets using Seth's plan.

2. Tell the size of chunk that helps you to "see" each fraction.

   a. $\dfrac{1}{4}$ b. $\dfrac{1}{10}$ c. $\dfrac{1}{20}$ d. $\dfrac{1}{5}$

3. Without splitting any of the areas into smaller areas, shade in the area corresponding to each of fractions named below.

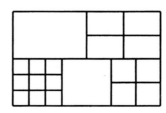

   a. $\dfrac{7}{16}$ b. $\dfrac{5}{8}$ c. $\dfrac{7}{18}$ d. $\dfrac{5}{12}$

4. Unitize each quantity in at least two different ways:

    a. 3 weeks =

    b. $.05 =

    c. 16 (half pints) =

    d. $1\frac{1}{2}$ dozen =

    e. 26 (quarter-miles) =

    f. 4 inches =

    g. 5 (5-packs) of gum =

    h. 17 pairs of shoelaces =

    i. 3 (8-packs) of soda =

5. Do this in your head: Which is the better buy: A 6-pack of cola for $ 1.89 or a 12-pack for $3.29?

6. Do this in your head: Notebook paper costs $1.89 for 500 sheets or $.99 for 250 sheets. Which is the better buy?

7. Do this in your head: A 10-pound bag of rice costs $5.50. A 15-pound bag costs $8.40. Which is the better buy?

8

Sharing and Comparing

Discussion of Activities

1. Before pushing tables together, on every table there were 2 candy bars for 3 people. After pushing the tables together, there were 8 candy bars for 12 people. In either arrangement, each student gets the same amount of candy, $\frac{2}{3}$ of a candy bar.

2. a. Partition each figure so that it has 6 equal pieces.

   b. Partition each figure so that it has 12 equal pieces.

   c. Partition the first figure into 9 equal pieces.

   d. Partition each figure so that it has 12 equal pieces.

   e. Partition each figure so that it has 20 equal pieces.

   f. Partition each figure so that it has 24 equal pieces.

3. a. Partition each figure so that it has 6 equal pieces. $\frac{2}{3}$ is longer by $\frac{1}{6}$.

   b. Partition each figure so that it has 24 equal pieces. $\frac{2}{3}$ is longer by $\frac{1}{24}$.

   c. Partition each figure so that it has 36 equal pieces. $\frac{1}{4}$ is longer by $\frac{1}{36}$.

   d. Partition each figure so that it has 24 equal pieces. $\frac{9}{12}$ is longer by $\frac{3}{24}$ or $\frac{1}{8}$.

   e. Partition each figure so that it has 24 equal pieces. $\frac{7}{8}$ is longer by $\frac{1}{24}$.

4. a. At Table A, each child gets 1 cookie. At Table B, each child gets $\frac{5}{4}$ cookies or $1\frac{1}{4}$ cookies. A child at Table B gets $\frac{1}{4}$ of a cookie more than a child at Table A.

   b. At Table A, each child gets $\frac{7}{3}$ cookies or $2\frac{1}{3}$ cookies. At Table B, each child gets 2 cookies. A child at Table A gets $\frac{1}{3}$ of a cookie more than a child at Table B.

   c. At Table A, each child gets $\frac{8}{3}$ cookies or $2\frac{2}{3}$ cookies. At Table B, each child gets $\frac{10}{4}$

cookies or $2\frac{1}{2}$ cookies. A child at Table A gets $\frac{1}{6}$ of a cookie more than a child at Table B.

d. This is fair.

e. At Table A, each child gets $\frac{1}{3}$ of a cookie. At Table B, each child gets $\frac{1}{4}$ of a cookie. A child at Table A gets $\frac{1}{12}$ of a cookie more than a child at Table B.

f. At Table A, each child gets $\frac{4}{3}$ cookies or $1\frac{1}{3}$ cookies. At Table B, each child gets $\frac{5}{4}$ cookies or $1\frac{1}{4}$ cookies. A child at Table A gets $\frac{1}{12}$ of a cookie more than a child at Table B.

g. At Table A, each child gets $\frac{2}{3}$ of a cookie. At Table B, each child gets $\frac{5}{4}$ cookies or $1\frac{1}{4}$ cookies. A child at Table B gets $\frac{7}{12}$ of a cookie more than a child at Table A.

5. a. Both pictures are divided into 3 equal pieces and show 1 shaded piece. Both show $\frac{1}{3}$.

b. The triangle is $\frac{1}{8}$ because 4 such equal triangles fit on each half of the figure. In the second figure, the piece marked is also $\frac{1}{8}$ because 8 such rectangles fit inside the square.

c. The areas are not equal. The first figure is divided into 3 equal pieces and the shaded amount is $\frac{1}{3}$. The second figure is divided into 4 equal pieces and 2 are shaded, so $\frac{2}{4}$ or $\frac{1}{2}$ is shaded.

d. The first figure is divided into 8 equal pieces, and 2 are shaded. So it shows $\frac{2}{8}$ or $\frac{1}{4}$. The second figure is divided into 4 equal parts and the shaded piece is $\frac{1}{4}$.

e. Both figures are divided into 4 equal pieces with 1 shaded, thus showing $\frac{1}{4}$. Both pieces do not look the same because one was divided horizontally and one vertically, but they are still equal in area.

f. In the first figure, $\frac{1}{2}$ is shaded. In the second figure, $\frac{2}{4}$ or $\frac{1}{2}$ is shaded.

g. Although divided differently, both rectangles have 1 of 6 equal pieces shaded and the pieces are equal in area. Both show $\frac{1}{6}$.

6. a. Each girl gets $1\frac{1}{2}$ pizzas. Each boy gets 1 pizza. A girl gets $\frac{1}{2}$ of a pizza more than a boy gets.

b. Each girl gets $\frac{1}{2}$ pizza. If we try to give each boy $\frac{1}{2}$ pizza, we are short by $\frac{1}{2}$ pizza. Each boy gets $\frac{1}{2} \div 7$ or $\frac{1}{14}$ of a pizza less than a girl. A girl gets $\frac{1}{14}$ of a pizza more than a boy gets.

c. Each girl gets $\frac{2}{5}$ of a pizza. If we try to give each boy $\frac{2}{5}$ of a pizza, we are short by $\frac{3}{5}$ of a pizza. Each boy gets $\frac{3}{5} \div 9$ or $\frac{1}{15}$ of a pizza less than a girl. A girl gets $\frac{1}{15}$ of a pizza more than a boy gets.

d. Each girl gets $\frac{1}{3}$ of a pizza. When we give each boy $\frac{1}{3}$ of a pizza, $1\frac{1}{3}$ pizzas are left over. When the 5 boys share the left-over pizza, each gets $\frac{4}{15}$ of a pizza more than a girl gets.

e. Each girl gets $\frac{4}{6}$ or $\frac{2}{3}$ of a pizza. If we try to give each boy $\frac{2}{3}$ of a pizza, we are short $\frac{1}{3}$ of a pizza. Each boy gets $\frac{1}{3} \div 5$ or $\frac{1}{15}$ of a pizza less than a girl gets. A girl gets $\frac{1}{15}$ of a pizza more than a boy gets.

7. Many young children use the word *half* when they see 2 pieces. They are not yet aware that the pieces must be the same size to be called halves. If the pieces she is seeing are not the same size, then they are not halves.

8. If each boy marks his piece so that it has 4 equal parts, he can then cut off 1 part and give it to the boy who just came along. Then everyone will have $\frac{3}{12}$ or $\frac{1}{4}$ of the original length.

9. a. $\frac{1}{6}$　　b. $\frac{1}{36}$　　c. $\frac{11}{12}$　　d. $1\frac{1}{12}$　　e. $\frac{31}{24}$ or $1\frac{7}{24}$

Supplementary Activities

1. Shade-to-compare activities can be very ineffective. Analyze the work of this third grade student. Then use the strips below to determine which fractional part is greater and by how much.

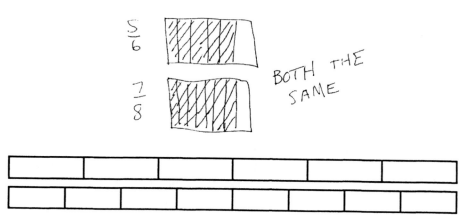

2. Twenty four people are going to Maria's Pizzeria for a birthday dinner. Two tables that seat 6 and three tables that seat 4 people have been prepared for this group. If they order 18 pizzas, how should the waiter distribute the pizzas at the 5 tables?

3. For a-d, visually determine how much food each person will get if they share equally. The gum is a 5-stick package.

   a.

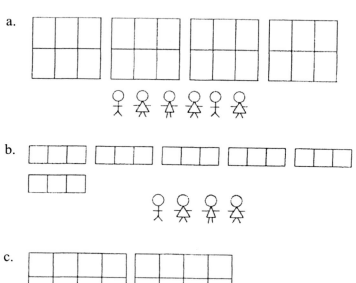

   b.

   c.

d.

4. Who gets more pizza, a girl or a boy? How much more?

5. For a–c below, decide who gets more pizza, a person seated at the table on the left, or a person seated at the table on the right. How much more pizza will each person at that table receive? Assume that all pizzas are the same size and type.

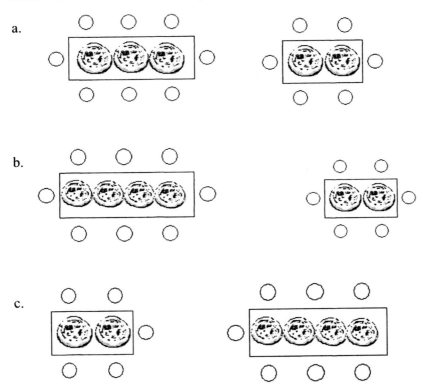

6. You are a bargain shopper. Would you rather have deal A or deal B? How much do you save (to the nearest cent)?

	Deal A	Deal B	How much do you save?
a.	$\frac{7}{10}$ lb for $.50	$\frac{3}{5}$ lb for $.50	
b.	$\frac{5}{6}$ lb for $1.80	$\frac{7}{9}$ lb for $1.80	
c.	$\frac{3}{4}$ lb for $1.65	$\frac{4}{5}$ lb for $1.60	
d.	$\frac{7}{8}$ lb for $2.40	$\frac{5}{6}$ lb for $2.44	

7. What do you think about this child's reasoning? How does it compare with the student reasoning in activity 1?

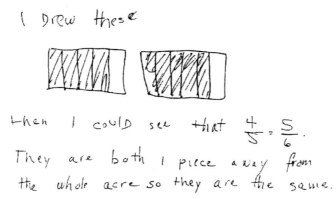

I Drew these

then I could see that $\frac{4}{5} = \frac{5}{6}$.
They are both 1 piece away from the whole acre so they are the same.

9

Proportional Reasoning

Discussion of Activities

1. a. If three pints cost $1.59, then 1 pint should cost $.53 ($\frac{1}{3}$ as much) and 4 should cost $2.12 (4 times the cost of 1). The milk cartons are priced proportionally. $\frac{2.12}{4} = \frac{.53}{1}$ and $\frac{1.59}{3} = \frac{.53}{1}$.

   b. This situation does not involve proportional or inversely proportional relationships. How long it takes to drive to the basketball game has nothing to do with how many people are in the car.

   c. The number of people is cut in half, which means that the work should take twice as long. This is the case, and the situation involves an inversely proportional relationship between the number of people and the time it takes to do a job.

   d. This situation does not involve any proportional or inversely proportional relationships. The number of sisters one boy has, has nothing to do with how many sisters another boy has.

   e. This situation does not involve any proportional or inversely proportional relationships. Time spent on solving a problem is not really dependent on where a person is solving it.

   f. If the number of eggs and the time it takes to eat them are proportional, then it should take 20 times as long to eat 20 eggs as it does to eat one egg. However, this is not the case. 1 egg per 20 seconds = 3 eggs per minute. The average rate for eating 20 eggs was 4 eggs per minute.

   g. Gallons of gas used and distance traveled are proportionally related. A full tank of gas (15 gallons) is $3\frac{1}{3}$ times $4\frac{1}{2}$ gallons and 333 miles is $3\frac{1}{3}$ times 100 miles, the distance traveled on $4\frac{1}{2}$ gallons.

   h. Amount spent and sales tax are proportionally related. When you spent $35 and paid $2.10 in sales tax, you spent 7 times as much as when you spent $5 and paid 7 times as much as you paid on sales tax.

2. a.

	# tickets	Profit	Notes
a	1	$1.15	given
b	100	115	100a
c	10	11.50	b ÷ 10
d	5	5.75	$\frac{1}{2}$c
e	20	23	2c
f	3	3.45	3a
g	128	147.20	b + d + e + f

The school makes $147.20 on 128 tickets.

b.

	# cans	Cost	Notes
a	1	$4.49	given
b	10	44.90	10a
c	5	22.45	$\frac{1}{2}$b
d	15	67.35	b + c

There is enough money to buy 15 cans.

c.

	Distance (km)	Time (min)	Notes
a	10	45	given
b	1	4.5	a ÷ 10
c	6	27	6b
d	.1	.45	b ÷ 10
e	.2	.90	2d
f	.01	.045	d ÷ 10
g	.05	.225	5f
h	6.25	28.125	c + e + g

It would take him just a little over 28 minutes.

3. a. 2875 words.

  b. $38.99

  c. 8 baseball caps.

  d. $414\frac{3}{8}$ miles.

  e. $45

  f. 9.8 quarts.

4. a. Diameter and area are not proportional.

diameter (feet)	area (sq. ft.)
3	7.06858
6	28.27433

x 2 (...) x 4

b. Distance and cost are not proportional.

distance (miles)	cost (dollars)
2	5.50
10	21.50
50	101.50

x 5 (...) x 3.91

x 5 (...) x 4.72

c. There is a proportional relationship between the length and the perimeter.

length (feet)	perimeter (feet)
3	9
9	27

x 3 (...) x 3

$$p = 3 \cdot 1$$

5. Hold the number of cords constant and find out how long it would take 4 men to cut them. Then hold the number of men constant and find the amount of time it would take them to cut 3 cords.

Men	8	4	4
Cords	9	9	3
Hours	6.5	13	$\frac{13}{3} = 4\frac{1}{3}$

6. Hold the time constant and figure out how many cars 14 robots can make. Then hold the robots constant and figure out how many cars they can make in 8 hours.

Robots	3	12	2	14	14
Cars	19	76	$\dfrac{76}{6}$	$76 + \dfrac{76}{6}$	$\dfrac{76}{5} + \dfrac{76}{30} = 17$
Hours	40	40	40	40	8

Note that the answer is greater than 17, but less than 18. Therefore we conclude that they can make 17 cars.

7. a. There is a proportional relationship between weight in pounds and weight in kilograms. In both of the instances given, the ratio of pounds to kilograms is about 2.20. We can express this in the equation $p = 2.2\,k$.

   b. There is a proportional relationship between the striking distance and the time until you hear the crash. The time in seconds at which the crash is heard is three times the distance in miles from where the lightning struck. We can express this in the equation $t = 3d$.

   c. There is a proportional relationship between the pressure on your ears and your distance under water. The pressure is .43 times the distance. We can express this in the equation $p = .43\,d$.

8. a. 1 horse will eat 15 pounds of hay in a month.

   b. 10 robots will produce 600 packages of auto parts in 10 hours.

   c. At the same rate, 24 hens will produce 384 eggs or 32 dozen eggs in 24 days.

Supplementary Activities

1. Solve by reasoning up and down.

    a. In 3 weeks, a horse eats 10 pounds of hay. How much will he eat in 5 weeks?

    b. A dragon's tail is $\frac{3}{4}$ of its total length. If the tail is $6\frac{3}{4}$ feet long, what is the total length of the dragon?

    c. Mary lost $\frac{3}{7}$ of her baseball cards. She has 16 left. How many did she lose?

    d. It takes Jim and his 2 brothers 4 hours to do the yard work. When one of the boys is sick, how long does it take the other two to do the work?

    e. You watch TV for $12\frac{1}{2}$ hours a week. How many hours do you watch in a year?

    f. It takes Steve $1\frac{1}{3}$ hours to mow his lawn. He spent 100 hours mowing last summer. How many times did he mow?

    g. A 12-person cleaning crew cleans a certain office building every night. It takes them 6 hours to complete the job. One night 2 people failed to show up for work. How long did it take the rest of the crew to finish the job?

    h. Mark studies $2\frac{3}{4}$ hours a week for each credit that he carries during a semester. This semester, he is taking 15 credits. How much time does he spend studying?

    i. The home improvement store has fencing for $16 for 2.5 lineal feet. You figure that it will take 110 feet of fencing to fence your garden. How much will it cost you?

    j. Jack drove 150 miles on 5 gallons of gas. How many gallons would his car use if he drove 225 miles?

    k. If it takes 15 hours to fill a swimming pool with one hose, how long will it take if I use 4 hoses (same hoses, water running at the same rate through each)?

    l. If it takes 3 painters 5 days to paint 3 houses, how long will it take 9 painters to paint them?

    m. At Camp Getaway, 5 boys use 3 bottles of shampoo in 2 weeks. At the same rate, how much shampoo will 30 boys use in a week?

2. Josh and Kristin are seventh grade students who are using reasoning to solve a fairly complex problem. See if you can figure out what they are doing. Also, account for the discrepancy in their answers.

    For every 50 people who attend the school fair, about 37 of them will purchase a raffle ticket in addition to paying the entrance fee. The school makes $1.25 profit on every raffle ticket. If 723 people have purchased tickets to the fair, how much money can the school hope to make on the raffle?

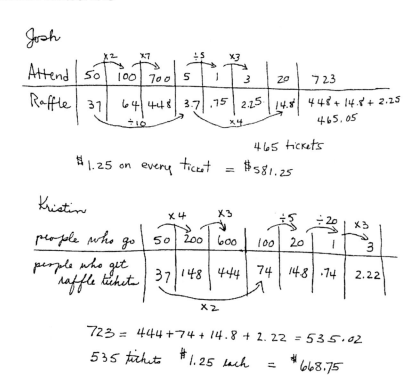

Josh

Attend	50	100	700	5	1	3	20	723
Raffle	37	64	448	3.7	.75	2.25	14.8	448 + 14.8 + 2.25

×2   ×7   ÷5   ×3
÷10   ×4

465.05

465 tickets

$1.25 on every ticket = $581.25

Kristin

people who go	50	200	600	100	20	1	3
people who get raffle tickets	37	148	444	74	14.8	.74	2.22

×4   ×3   ÷5   ÷20   ×3
×2

723 = 444 + 74 + 14.8 + 2.22 = 535.02

535 tickets $1.25 each = $668.75

3. Grandma has some special plant food that comes in powder form. The directions say to mix 2.5 teaspoons with 8 ounces of water. There are 8 teaspoonfuls left, and I am going to mix it all up. How much water should I add?

4. Sam, amateur detective, was walking along at the rate of about $3\frac{1}{2}$ mph when a car passed him on the road and tossed a gun out the window. He heard sirens back in town and immediately suspected that it was a get-away car. He counted his steps—29 in all—until the car turned the corner and he lost sight of it. It took him another 203 steps to get to the corner, but by then, the car was gone. He told the police that he was not sure it was the get-away car because it was not moving very quickly. How did Sam know how fast the car was moving?

5. Candy costs $8.40 a pound. Mr. Kennedy bought 37 (1-pound) boxes for his employees. How much did it cost him?

6. Another chicken problem. A chicken and a half lays an egg and a half in a day and a half. How many dozen eggs do 12 chickens lay in 12 days?

7. If 3 robots can assemble 17 cars in 10 minutes, how many cars can 14 robots assemble in 45 minutes?

8. Return to chapter 1 and solve the Lewis Carroll problem.

10

Reasoning with Fractions

Discussion of Activities

1. A method is suggested for each problem; however, in some cases, other methods may be used.

   a. CRP $\frac{8}{14}$ is greater than $\frac{1}{2}$ and $\frac{4}{9}$ is less than $\frac{1}{2}$. So $\frac{8}{14} > \frac{4}{9}$.

   b. $\frac{4}{9}$ unit fractions

   c. SNP $\frac{3}{17}$ and $\frac{3}{19}$ each have the same number of pieces, and so the critical question becomes, "What size are the pieces?" Seventeenths are larger than nineteenths, so $\frac{3}{17} > \frac{3}{19}$.

   d. $\frac{11}{21}$ CRP($\frac{1}{2}$)

   e. SSP $\frac{8}{13}$ All of the pieces are the same size, so if you have 8 of them you have more than if you have 5 of them. $\frac{8}{13} > \frac{5}{13}$.

   f. $\frac{5}{8}$ CRP($\frac{1}{2}$)

   g. CRP $\frac{3}{2}$ is $\frac{1}{2}$ greater than 1, but $\frac{4}{3}$ is only $\frac{1}{3}$ greater than 1. $\frac{3}{2} > \frac{4}{3}$.

   h. $\frac{5}{11}$ CRP($\frac{1}{2}$)

   i. $\frac{2}{3}$ SNP

   j. $\frac{4}{9}$ unit fractions

   k. $\frac{7}{9}$ CRP($\frac{1}{2}$)

   l. $\frac{7}{12}$ CRP($\frac{1}{2}$)

   m. $\frac{7}{8}$ CRP(1)

o. $\frac{1}{5}$ SNP

n. $\frac{3}{7}$ CRP$(\frac{1}{2})$

p. $\frac{5}{9}$ CRP$(\frac{1}{2})$

q. $\frac{3}{4}$ unit fractions: $\frac{5}{9} = \frac{1}{3} + \frac{1}{9} + \frac{1}{9}$ $\frac{3}{4} = \frac{1}{3} + \frac{1}{6} + \frac{1}{4}$ Both fractions contain $\frac{1}{3}$, but the remaining fractions composing $\frac{3}{4}$ are greater than the remaining fractions in $\frac{5}{9}$

$\frac{3}{4} > \frac{5}{9}$.

r. $\frac{10}{11}$ CRP(1)

s. $\frac{3}{5}$ CRP$(\frac{1}{2})$

t. $\frac{13}{14}$ CRP(1)

2. a. $\frac{7}{8} = \frac{1}{3} + \frac{1}{6} + \frac{1}{4} + \frac{1}{8}$ $\frac{3}{5} = \frac{1}{5} + \frac{1}{5} + \frac{1}{10} + \frac{1}{10}$ $\frac{7}{8} > \frac{3}{5}$

b. $\frac{7}{8} = \frac{1}{2} + \frac{1}{4} + \frac{1}{8}$ $\frac{5}{6} = \frac{1}{2} + \frac{1}{4} + \frac{1}{12}$ $\frac{7}{8} > \frac{5}{6}$

c. $\frac{7}{8} = \frac{1}{2} + \frac{1}{3} + \frac{1}{24}$ $\frac{9}{10} = \frac{1}{2} + \frac{1}{3} + \frac{1}{15}$ $\frac{9}{10} > \frac{7}{8}$

3. a. Write $\frac{1}{6}$ as $1 \div 6$ and $\frac{1}{5}$ as $\frac{6}{5} \div 6$. Then any fractions between 1 and $1\frac{1}{5}$ (all divided by 6 will be in between $\frac{1}{6}$ and $\frac{1}{5}$. For example, $\frac{1\frac{1}{6}}{6} = \frac{7}{36}$, $\frac{1\frac{1}{7}}{6} = \frac{8}{42}$, and $\frac{1\frac{1}{8}}{6} = \frac{9}{48}$.

b. $\frac{1}{13} = \frac{14}{13} \div 14 = 1\frac{1}{13} \div 14$, so $\frac{7}{13} = \frac{7\frac{7}{13}}{14}$. To find fractions between $\frac{7}{14}$ and $\frac{7\frac{7}{13}}{14}$ choose numerators greater than 7 and less than $7\frac{7}{13}$. For example, choose $7\frac{6}{13}$, $7\frac{5}{13}$, and

$7\frac{4}{13}$. Then $\frac{7\frac{6}{13}}{14} = \frac{97}{182}$ and $\frac{7\frac{5}{13}}{14} = \frac{96}{182}$ and $\frac{7\frac{4}{13}}{14} = \frac{95}{182}$ are between the given fractions.

c. To obtain fractions between $\frac{6}{8}$ and $\frac{7}{8}$, choose numerators between 6 and 7, say $6\frac{1}{3}$, $6\frac{1}{4}$, and $6\frac{1}{5}$. Then $\frac{6\frac{1}{3}}{8} = \frac{9}{24}$, $\frac{6\frac{1}{4}}{8} = \frac{25}{32}$, and $\frac{6\frac{1}{5}}{8} = \frac{31}{40}$ are between the given fractions.

4. a. To construct the smallest possible sum, you will need the larger numbers in the denominators, so make one denominator 7 and the other 8. Then put the 6 with the 8 so that you get a larger number of smaller pieces.

$$\frac{5}{7} + \frac{6}{8}$$

b. To construct the largest possible sum, you will need pieces of larger size, so use 5 and 6 as denominators. Make 8 the numerator for the 5 so that you get a larger number of larger pieces.

$$\frac{8}{5} + \frac{7}{6}$$

c. To construct the smallest positive difference, you want to make the fractions as close as possible in size and you want the largest numbers in the denominator so that your difference is very small. $\frac{5}{8} < \frac{6}{7}$, so put 6 as the numerator above 8.

$$\frac{6}{8} - \frac{5}{7}$$

d. To construct the largest difference, first create the largest fraction, and then with the remaining numbers, the smallest fraction.

$$\frac{8}{5} - \frac{6}{7}$$

e. To construct the smallest possible product, choose the denominators to give the smallest-size pieces. After you choose 8 and 7 as denominators, it does not matter which numerator is 5 and which is 6.

$$\frac{5}{8} \times \frac{6}{7} \text{ or } \frac{6}{8} \times \frac{5}{7}$$

f. To construct the largest possible product, you want the largest possible numerators, so choose 8 and 7. Then 5 and 6 may be placed in either of the denominators.

$$\frac{8}{6} \times \frac{7}{5} \text{ or } \frac{8}{5} \times \frac{7}{6}$$

g. To construct the smallest quotient, the divisor should be as large as possible, so choose $\frac{8}{5}$ as the divisor. Then the dividend should be as small as possible.

$$\frac{6}{7} \div \frac{8}{5}$$

h. To construct the largest quotient, the dividend should be as large as possible, so choose $\frac{8}{5}$. The divisor should be as small as possible.

$$\frac{8}{5} \div \frac{6}{7}$$

5. a. The fraction gets larger.

b. You cannot tell.

c. The fraction gets smaller.

d. The fractions are equivalent.

6. There is a difference of $\frac{3}{5}$ and we need 3 fractions (4 equal spaces) between $\frac{2}{5}$ and 1. This means that the spaces between the fractions will be $\frac{3}{20}$. Obtain the fractions by adding $\frac{3}{20}$, $\frac{6}{20}$, and $\frac{9}{20}$, respectively, to $\frac{2}{5}$. The fractions are $\frac{11}{20}$, $\frac{14}{20}$, and $\frac{17}{20}$.

Supplementary Problems

1. Decide which of the two fractions in each pair represents a larger amount using reasoning only. No common denominators or cross multiplying strategies are to be used.

   a. $\dfrac{3}{7}, \dfrac{5}{8}$ c. $\dfrac{4}{9}, \dfrac{5}{11}$ e. $\dfrac{3}{8}, \dfrac{5}{9}$ g. $\dfrac{6}{11}, \dfrac{7}{12}$

   b. $\dfrac{3}{7}, \dfrac{2}{5}$ d. $\dfrac{2}{5}, \dfrac{5}{9}$ f. $\dfrac{3}{7}, \dfrac{5}{12}$

2. One of our third grade students, who was shading to compare $\dfrac{3}{8}$ and $\dfrac{4}{9}$, observed that he could use this drawing to add the fractions $\dfrac{3}{8}$ and $\dfrac{4}{9}$. He said he would add up all the shaded blocks, and subtract off the ones that have two kinds of shading because otherwise, they would get counted twice. What do you think about his strategy?

$$\frac{3}{8} + \frac{4}{9} =$$ 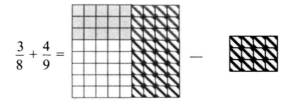 $$-$$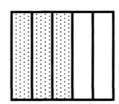

3. Answer the following *Can You See* questions using this figure.

   a. Can you see $\dfrac{3}{5}$ of something?

   b. Can you see $\dfrac{5}{3}$ of something?

   c. Can you see $\dfrac{2}{3}$ of $\dfrac{3}{5}$?

   d. Can you see $\dfrac{5}{3}$ of $\dfrac{3}{5}$?

   e. Can you see $1 \div \dfrac{3}{5}$?

f. Can you see $\dfrac{3}{5} \div 2$?

g. Can you see $\dfrac{5}{4} \div \dfrac{3}{4}$?

4. Use Martin's method to find three fractions between

a. $\dfrac{1}{8}$ and $\dfrac{1}{7}$

b. $\dfrac{2}{5}$ and 1

c. $1\dfrac{3}{7}$ and $1\dfrac{1}{2}$

5. Find 3 equally spaced fractions between

a. 1 and $1\dfrac{1}{5}$

b. $\dfrac{3}{7}$ and $\dfrac{6}{7}$

c. $2\dfrac{1}{3}$ and $2\dfrac{3}{4}$

6. A fourth grade student was trying to find a fraction that was half way between $\dfrac{1}{3}$ and $\dfrac{1}{2}$.

Analyze her method then use it to find the fraction half way between $\dfrac{3}{4}$ and $\dfrac{7}{8}$.

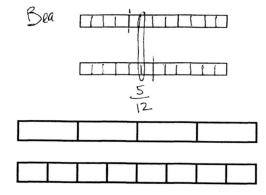

Bea

$\dfrac{5}{12}$

11

Part-Whole Comparisons

Discussion of Activities

1. a. The triangles are 4 of the 9 items in the group: $\frac{4}{9}$

   b. The unit is the entire group of figures.

   c. Two triangles are half the set of four triangles: $\frac{2}{4} = \frac{1}{2}$

   d. In this case, the question makes it clear that the unit is the set of 4 triangles, not the entire set of figures.

   e. Three circles compared to the number of circles in the set is $\frac{3}{5}$.

   f. The set of 5 circles is explicitly named as the unit.

2. a. $\frac{3}{5}$ (days)　　　　b. $\frac{12}{1}$ (pair)　　　　c. $\frac{1}{12}$ (pair)

   d. $\frac{\frac{8}{12}}{1}$ (12-pack)　　e. $\frac{1\frac{1}{3}}{1}$ (6-packs)　　f. $\frac{1\frac{1}{2}}{1}$ (half dollars)

   g. $\frac{4\frac{1}{4}}{1}$ (acres)　　　h. $\frac{8\frac{1}{2}}{1}$ (half acres)

3. a.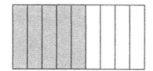

   b.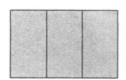

   4 acres $= 12\left(\frac{1}{3}\text{-acres}\right)$ and 6 equal parts each contain 2 of the $\frac{1}{3}$ pieces. Shade 5 out of 6 of the $\left(\frac{2}{3}\text{-acres}\right)$ pieces.

c.

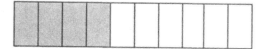

10 acres = 5 (pair of acres). Shade 2 out of the 5 (pairs of acres).

d.

2 cakes = $6\left(\frac{1}{3}\text{-cakes}\right)$. Shade 5 of the $6\left(\frac{1}{3}\text{-cakes}\right)$.

e.

2 cupcakes = $4\left(\frac{1}{2}\text{-cupcakes}\right)$. To shade 7 out of $4\left(\frac{1}{2}\text{-cupcakes}\right)$, you need another copy of the unit (2 cupcakes).

4. The area of the square is $A = s^2$ or 25 sq. ft. The area of the circle is $A = \pi r^2$ or 4π sq. ft. The part of the square covered by the circle is $\frac{4\pi}{25} = .5026$ or just a little over half the square.

5. $\frac{4}{5}$(parts) $= \frac{24}{30}(\frac{1}{6}\text{-parts})$ and $\frac{5}{6}$(parts) $= \frac{25}{30}(\frac{1}{5}\text{-parts})$ so $\frac{5}{6}$ is larger by $\frac{1}{30}$ of an acre.

6. Note that in this problem, the unit is the set of 18 stars. Think about what each fraction means in relation to that unit.

a. 18 stars = 3(6-packs). Therefore, $\frac{2}{3}$ is 2 out of 3 (6-packs) or 12 stars.

b. 18 stars = 6 (3-packs). $\frac{5}{6}$ is 5 of 6 (3-packs) or 15 stars.

c. 18 stars = 9(pair). $\frac{7}{9}$ is 7 out of 9 (pair) or 14 stars.

d. 18 stars = $12\left(1\frac{1}{2}\text{-packs}\right)$. $\frac{7}{12}$ is 7 out of $12\left(1\frac{1}{2}\text{-packs}\right)$ or $10\frac{1}{2}$ stars.

e. $\frac{11}{18}$ is 11 out of 18 single stars or 11 stars.

7. a. $\frac{2}{3}$ (parts) $= \frac{10}{15}\left(\frac{1}{5}\text{-parts}\right)$ and $\frac{3}{5}$ (parts) $= \frac{9}{15}\left(\frac{1}{3}\text{-parts}\right)$, so $\frac{2}{3} > \frac{3}{5}$.

b. $\frac{5}{6}$ (parts)$= \frac{15}{18}\left(\frac{1}{3}\text{-parts}\right)$ and $\frac{7}{9}$ (parts) $= \frac{14}{18}\left(\frac{1}{3}\text{-parts}\right)$, so $\frac{5}{6} > \frac{7}{9}$.

c. $\frac{3}{4}$ (parts) $= \frac{15}{20} \left(\frac{1}{5}\text{-parts} \right)$ and $\frac{7}{10} = \frac{14}{20}$ (halves), so $\frac{3}{4} > \frac{7}{10}$.

8. $\frac{5}{6}$ (3-packs) = 15 hearts. $\frac{2}{3}$ (6-packs) = 12 hearts. $\frac{5}{9}$ (pair) = 10 hearts. Therefore, $\frac{5}{6} > \frac{2}{3}$ $> \frac{5}{9}$.

9. $\frac{7}{8}$ (5-packs) = 35

10. $\frac{1}{4}$ (parts) $= \frac{3}{12} \left(\frac{1}{3}\text{-parts} \right)$ and $\frac{1}{3}$ (parts) $= \frac{4}{12} \left(\frac{1}{4}\text{-parts} \right)$, so Roger has $2\frac{3}{12}$ and he gives Paul $1\frac{4}{12}$. Use a strip to see that he will have $\frac{11}{12}$ left.

11. Using the equivalent names from question 10, you can see that Maurice has $2\frac{8}{12}$ and Sam has $3\frac{3}{12}$. Together they have $2\frac{8}{12} + 3\frac{3}{12} = 5\frac{11}{12}$.

12. What is $1\frac{2}{9} \div 1\frac{2}{3}$? How many copies of $1\frac{2}{3}$ can I measure out of $1\frac{2}{9}$? $1\frac{2}{3} = \frac{5}{3}$ (parts) $= \frac{15}{9} \left(\frac{1}{3}\text{-parts} \right)$ and $1\frac{2}{9}$ is $\frac{11}{9}$ (parts). How many times can you measure 15 parts out of 11 parts? $\frac{11}{15}$ (less than once).

13. I can think of 4 parts as $20\left(\frac{1}{5}\text{-parts} \right)$. One copy of that would be $20\left(\frac{1}{5}\text{-parts} \right)$ and $\frac{1}{5}$ of the 20 parts is another 4 parts, so we have $24\left(\frac{1}{5}\text{-parts} \right)$ or $4\frac{4}{5}$.

14. What is $2\frac{1}{3} \div 1\frac{1}{4}$? How many copies of $1\frac{1}{4}$ can I measure out of $2\frac{1}{3}$? $2\frac{1}{3} = \frac{7}{3}$ (parts) $= \frac{28}{12} \left(\frac{1}{4}\text{-parts} \right)$ and $1\frac{1}{4}$ is $\frac{5}{4}$ (parts) $= \frac{15}{12} \left(\frac{1}{3}\text{-parts} \right)$. How many times can you measure 15 parts out of 28 parts? $1\frac{13}{15}$ times.

Supplementary Problems

1. 10 cents is what part of a dollar? Find 3 different ways to name the part of a dollar.

2. Use this set of diamonds to order these fractions from smallest to largest:

$$\frac{7}{9}, \frac{4}{3}, \frac{5}{9}, \frac{1}{2}$$

3. Using the methods of this chapter, draw pictures to show each quantity.

   a. I had 3 cakes, and $\frac{5}{6}$ of them were eaten. How much cake was eaten?

   b. I own 5 acres and $\frac{7}{15}$ of my property is covered by a lake. How many acres are covered by water?

   c. I had 32 hard candies, but I have only $\frac{3}{8}$ of them left. How many are left?

   d. I have 2 acres of land and $\frac{3}{4}$ of it is wooded. How many acres are wooded?

4. The numerator of a part-whole comparison is a counting number. Does it count
   a. the number of pieces in a share?
   b. the total number of shares?
   c. the total number of pieces in the designated shares?
   d. the number of objects in the unit?
   e. a designated number of shares?

5. The denominator of a part-whole comparison tells what is being counted. Does it refer to
   a. the number of pieces in a share?
   b. the total number of shares?
   c. the total number of pieces in the designated shares?
   d. the number of objects in the unit?
   e. a designated number of shares?

6. Draw an appropriate picture to show each operation and write the division problem symbolically ($a \div b = c$).

   a. How many $\frac{1}{2}$'s are there in 8?

   b. How many times you can measure $\frac{2}{3}$ out of 3?

7. Shade $\frac{5}{6}$ of this rectangle and name as many equivalent fractions as you can see.

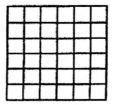

8. Two students responded to this question: Which is more, $\frac{3}{5}$ of a pie or $\frac{7}{11}$ of a pie? Are their answers correct?

A.

$$\frac{3 \text{ pies}}{5 \text{ pies}} = \frac{21 \ (\frac{1}{7} \text{ pies})}{35 \ (\frac{1}{7} \text{ pies})}$$

$$\frac{7 \text{ pies}}{11 \text{ pies}} = \frac{21 \ (\frac{1}{3} \text{ pies})}{33 \ (\frac{1}{3} \text{ pies})}$$

The first person and the second person have the same number of pieces but the first one has smaller pieces so he has less pie. ¿☺

B.

⑪ ⑪ ⑪
⑪ ⑪ ⑪ ⑪ ⑪ $\frac{33}{55}$

⑤ ⑤ ⑤ ⑤ ⑤ ⑤ ⑤
⑤ ⑤ ⑤ ⑤ ⑤ ⑤ ⑤ ⑤ ⑤ ⑤ ⑤   This guy has

more ↙
$\frac{35}{55}$

9. Solve by unitizing.

   a. Which is larger, $\frac{5}{6}$ of a cake or $\frac{2}{3}$ of a cake?

   b. $\frac{4}{5}$ of a pizza or $\frac{5}{6}$ of a pizza?

   c. $\frac{2}{3}$ of an acre or $\frac{3}{5}$ of an acre?

   d. $\frac{5}{6}$ of a mile or $\frac{7}{9}$ of a mile?

   e. $\frac{3}{4}$ of a cherry pie or $\frac{7}{10}$ of the same pie?

10. Two candles of equal length are lighted at the same time. One candle takes 9 hours to burn out and the other takes 6 hours to burn out. After how much time will the slower-burning candle be exactly twice as long as the faster-burning candle?

12

Partitioning and Quotients

Discussion of Activities

1. d

2. b

3. The children all proposed to give each person $1\frac{1}{3}$ candy bars, but they also proposed different ways of breaking the candy bars. In each case, one share of the candy looks different and is named by different fractions:

$$\frac{1}{3} + \frac{1}{3} + \frac{1}{3} + \frac{1}{3}$$
$$\frac{1}{2} + \frac{1}{2} + \frac{2}{6}$$
$$\frac{1}{2} + \frac{1}{2} + \frac{1}{3}$$
$$\frac{2}{6} + \frac{2}{6} + \frac{2}{6} + \frac{2}{6}$$

Based on these partitions, the following fractions must be equivalent:

$$\frac{2}{6} = \frac{1}{3}$$
$$\frac{4}{3} = \frac{8}{6}$$
$$\frac{4}{3} = \frac{8}{6} = 1\frac{2}{6} = 1\frac{1}{3}$$

4. Each person will eat $\frac{4}{5}$ of a cake, which is $\frac{1}{5}$ of the total cakes.

5. One share will be $\frac{2}{4}$ or $\frac{1}{2}$ of a 6-pack. Each share is $\frac{1}{4}$ of the unit.

6. Student B used the least sophisticated strategy. The student split apart every 6-pack to make individual cans and then distributed them to the 3 children. Student C used the most sophisticated strategy because he or she used the least amount of cutting (separat-

ing) and marking. This student merely distributed entire 6-packs as far as possible, then distributed individual cans as necessary. Student A's strategy is between the other two in sophistication. Although Student A distributed 6-packs, he or she needed to mark the individual components of the 6-packs. Notice how the student drew each individual can within the 6-pack. This need to mark individual components of a composite unit is usually a sign that a student is in a transitional stage: he or she is beginning to think in terms of composite units, but still needs some visual reassurance that each person is getting the same number of cans.

7. Figure out the number of cuts that it would take to accomplish each of the partitions. Student A's strategy requires 6 cuts; B's requires 4 cuts; C's requires 10 cuts; and D's requires 8 cuts. You can see that Students A and B anticipated that a share would consist of 4 small rectangles, and they made some effort to keep each share connected. Students C and D were unable to anticipate that a share would consist of 4 rectangles, so they started by distributing 1 or 2 at a time. Ranking by sophistication (connectedness of shares), we get B, A, D, and C, from highest to lowest.

8.

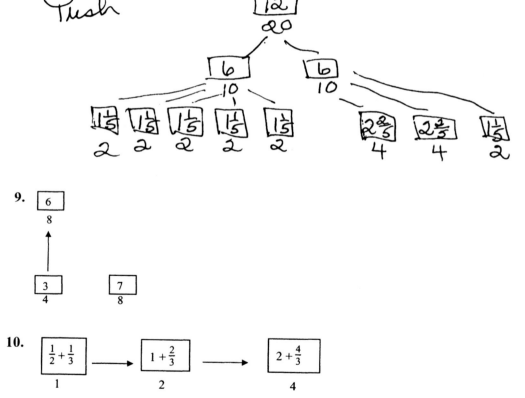

9. $\boxed{\dfrac{6}{8}}$

$\uparrow$

$\boxed{\dfrac{3}{4}}$ $\boxed{\dfrac{7}{8}}$

10. $\boxed{\dfrac{1}{2} + \dfrac{1}{3}}$ $\longrightarrow$ $\boxed{1 + \dfrac{2}{3}}$ $\longrightarrow$ $\boxed{2 + \dfrac{4}{3}}$

1   2   4

Four people get more than 2 pizzas, so they cannot be sitting at a table where 5 people share 2 pizzas.

11. Yes. It was fair. Here is Dan's work for this problem.

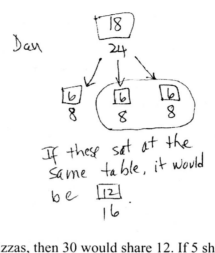

12. If 5 people shared 2 pizzas, then 30 would share 12. If 5 share 1 cheese pizza, then 30 would share 6. So there must have been 12 veggie pizzas and 6 cheese pizzas.

13. $\boxed{3 + 4}$ for 8 means we each got $\dfrac{3}{8} + \dfrac{1}{2}$ which is like $\dfrac{7}{8}$.

14. Four people sharing 1 pizza is like 16 sharing 4. Two people sharing 1 pizza is like 16 sharing 8. So there must have been 4 cheese pizzas and 8 pepperoni pizzas for 16 people.

$$\frac{\boxed{4 + 8}}{16} \quad = \quad \frac{\boxed{1 + 2}}{4} \quad = \quad \frac{\boxed{\dfrac{1}{2} + 1}}{2}$$

The 2 people got half a cheese pizza and 1 pepperoni pizza.

15. Here is Prem's solution to $\dfrac{2}{3} + \dfrac{1}{4}$.

Supplementary Problems

1. Alice and Brad will share a large cookie. Is there a way to partition the cookie so that one child gets two pieces and the other child gets three pieces, but they both get the same amount?

2. If 4 people share 6 candy bars, how much candy will each receive?

3. If 4 people share 6 candy bars, how much of the candy will each receive?

4. Here are some results you obtained from the children in your class as they considered what one share would be when 4 people shared three identical pizzas. What addition statements could you make by visually unitizing these statements?

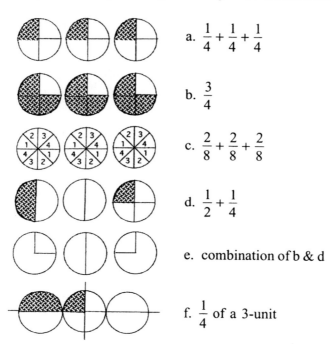

a. $\frac{1}{4} + \frac{1}{4} + \frac{1}{4}$

b. $\frac{3}{4}$

c. $\frac{2}{8} + \frac{2}{8} + \frac{2}{8}$

d. $\frac{1}{2} + \frac{1}{4}$

e. combination of b & d

f. $\frac{1}{4}$ of a 3-unit

5. Three people share the following candy bars. Show three different partitions, write the fractions to represent the pieces in each share, and note the equivalencies.

6. If 3 people share these candy bars, how much will one share be? What part of the unit is each share?

7. Eight people share 6 cheese and 4 mushroom pizzas. How much of each type of pizza is in a share? How much of the total pizza does each person get?

8. Suppose three girls share 3 pepperoni pizzas and 4 cheese pizzas. How much will each person get? If each of them takes her portion home and later shares it with her sister, how much will each girl eat?

9. Someone in my office had a birthday and so the boss took all 16 people out for pizza. He ordered 20 pizzas. At the restaurant, people sat at 1 table for 8, and the rest at booths for 2. How much pizza should the waiter deliver to each table and to each booth?

10. Who gets more pizza and how much more, 6 people sharing 9 pizzas, or 5 people sharing 8?

11. Could someone who was served $\frac{1}{2}$ pizza A $+ \frac{1}{4}$ pizza B $+ \frac{1}{3}$ pizza C be sitting at a table where 6 people are sharing 10 pizzas?

12. A group of 24 people ordered some pizzas. One of the people was served $\frac{1}{2}$ of a veggie pizza and $\frac{1}{6}$ of a cheese pizza. What must have been the group order?

13. How much is $\frac{2}{5} - \frac{1}{3}$?

14. Twelve people ordered some pizzas. One person got $\frac{1}{4}$ of a veggie pizza and $\frac{1}{2}$ of a cheese pizza. What must have been the group order? If that person was sitting at a table for 4, how many pizzas and of what type were delivered to his table?

13

Rational Numbers as Operators

Discussion of Activities

1. $\frac{3}{12}$ or $\frac{1}{4}$ because $\frac{1}{3} \cdot \frac{3}{4} = \frac{3}{12} = \frac{1}{4}$.

2. a. In each case, the system name is $\dfrac{\text{final output}}{\text{initial input}}$. You should get $1, \dfrac{2}{20} = \dfrac{1}{10}, \dfrac{9}{2}, \dfrac{24}{9} = \dfrac{8}{3}$, and $\dfrac{12}{24} = \dfrac{1}{2}$.

   b. Multiplying inverse operators gives 1; the system name is the product of the machine names.

3.

Input	Output
12	8
18	12
9	6
6	4
1	2/3

4. If $\frac{5}{9}$ of the teachers are female, $\frac{4}{9}$ are male. If $\frac{3}{8}$ of the males are single, then $\frac{3}{8} \cdot \frac{4}{9} = \frac{1}{6}$ are single males. If $\frac{1}{3}$ of the single males are over 50, $\frac{2}{3}$ are under 50. So $\frac{2}{3} \cdot \frac{1}{6} = \frac{1}{9}$ are single males under 50.

5. a. $\frac{3}{6}(8) = 4$ b. $\frac{3}{2}(2) = 3$ c. $4\left(\frac{2}{3}\right)(6) = 16$

6.

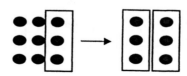

7. The first machine is a 1-for-2, so its label should be $\frac{1}{2}$. The second label is $\frac{1}{5}$. Even though their outputs are the same, they are performing different functions.

8. a. $\frac{1}{2} \cdot \frac{5}{6} \cdot 2 = \frac{10}{12} = \frac{5}{6}$ **b.** $\frac{2}{3} \cdot \frac{1}{6} = \frac{2}{18} = \frac{1}{9}$ **c.** $\frac{1}{2} \cdot \frac{1}{5} = \frac{2}{20} = \frac{1}{10}$ **d.** $\frac{1}{4} \cdot \frac{1}{3} = \frac{1}{12}$

9. 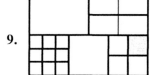 $\frac{1}{4} \cdot \frac{1}{3} \cdot \frac{1}{2} = \frac{1}{24}$

10. a. $\frac{3}{9} \cdot \frac{1}{3} \cdot \frac{1}{2} = \frac{1}{18}$ **b.** $\frac{2}{4} \cdot \frac{1}{2} \cdot \frac{1}{2} = \frac{2}{16} = \frac{1}{8}$ **c.** $\frac{1}{3} \cdot \frac{1}{2} = \frac{1}{6}$

11. a. $\frac{3}{8}$ 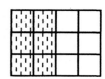   **b.** $\frac{4}{5}$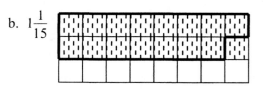

c. $\frac{1}{2}$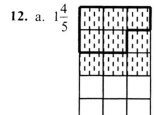

12. a. $1\frac{4}{5}$    **b.** $1\frac{1}{15}$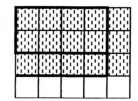

c. $4\frac{3}{8}$

d. $1\frac{9}{24}$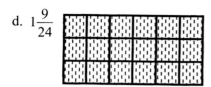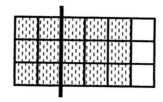

13. Ask yourself: What is the operator? operator $= \frac{\text{output}}{\text{input}} = \frac{\text{ILS}}{\text{US}} = \frac{1}{.2239}$. Then $\frac{1}{.2239}$ (50)

= 223.31 ILS.

14. The operator is $\frac{.161}{1}$. The operator operates on 50 ZAR to give $8.05 US.

15. The number of children is $\frac{1}{3}$ of the total, so the number of adults must be 32. The

women are $\frac{1}{4}$ of the adults, so there are 8 women. That leaves 24 men.

16. What operator changes $\frac{360}{100}$ to $\frac{220}{100}$? $\left(\quad \right) \cdot \frac{360}{100} = \frac{220}{100}$

If we divide by 360 and multiply by 220, we get $\frac{220}{360} = \frac{11}{18} = 61.11\%$

17. Think in term of what you pay. Yesterday you paid $\frac{50}{65}$. Today you will pay 90% of

yesterday's price. So you will pay $\frac{90}{100} \cdot \frac{50}{65} = \frac{9}{13}$. If you pay $\frac{9}{13}$ of the original price,

then $\frac{4}{13}$ is the discount. $\frac{4}{13} = 30.77\%$

18. a. Begin with 100. After a decrease of 10%, you have 90. 15% of 90 is 13.5. Therefore, you end up with 90 + 13.5 = 103.5 or 103.5% of your original amount.
b. 10% of 110 = 11. So you will have 110 – 11 = 99 or 99% of your original amount.
c. 60% of 50 = 30. You will have 50 + 30 = 80 or 80% of your original amount.
d. 50% of 120 = 60. You will have 120 – 60 = 60 or 60% of your original amount.
e. 25% of 70 = 17.5. You will have 70 + 17.5 = 87.5 or 87.5% of your original amount.

19. After folding both papers, you should see $\frac{8}{12}$ and $\frac{9}{12}$, respectively.

20. There are a number of possibilities. Here is one:

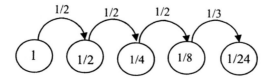

21. a. The operator is $\dfrac{6}{\frac{4}{3}} = \dfrac{18}{4}$. $\dfrac{18}{4}$ (6) = 27 doughnuts.

b. The operator is $\dfrac{\frac{2}{3}}{6} = \dfrac{1}{9}$. $\dfrac{1}{9}$ (21) $= \dfrac{21}{9} = 2\dfrac{1}{3}$ pizzas.

c. The operator is $\dfrac{10}{\frac{1}{4}} = 40$. 40(3) = 120 peanuts.

d. The operator is $\dfrac{2}{5}$. $\dfrac{2}{5}$ (6) $= 2\dfrac{2}{5}$ peach pies.

Supplementary Activities

1.   Shade in $\frac{1}{6}$ of the shaded part of this picture.

What is $\frac{1}{6}$ of $\frac{3}{4}$?

2.   Show $\frac{3}{4} \div \frac{3}{8}$.

What is $\frac{3}{4} \div \frac{3}{8}$?

3. Reducing a unit to half its size and then tripling the result in size is equivalent to _____.

4. Dividing something into 5 equal shares and then quadrupling one share is equivalent to _____.

5. Make a picture showing a 2-for-3 machine with an input of 12 items and another picture of an 8-for-12 machine with an input of 12 items. What is the output of each machine? Name some other machines that will have the same output.

6. Draw a picture to illustrate the action of a 5-for-6 operator on a 3-for-4 operator on this set of objects:

7. Write the name of the shaded area as a product of fractions.

a. 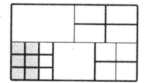 b. 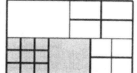 c.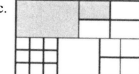

8. Find the number of children who are girls if you know that there are 12 male adults.

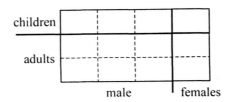

9. Fold one unit sheet of paper into thirds. Shade $\frac{1}{3}$.

   Fold another unit of the same size into fourths. Shade $\frac{1}{4}$.

   Continue to fold each unit until you have twelfths.
   What conclusions can you draw?

10. Fold two paper units until you can rename each of these fractions with the same denominator:

$$\frac{3}{8} \text{ and } \frac{1}{6}$$

11. Complete each diagram and carry out the paper folding that will result in the smallest fraction.

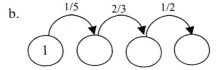

12. Can you see $\frac{3}{4}$ of $\frac{1}{2}$ of $\frac{1}{2}$? Shade it and then name the product $\frac{3}{4} \cdot \frac{1}{2} \cdot \frac{1}{2}$.

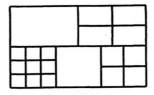

13. Can you see $\frac{2}{3}$ of $\frac{1}{3}$ of $\frac{1}{2}$? Shade it and then name the product $\frac{2}{3} \cdot \frac{1}{3} \cdot \frac{1}{2}$.

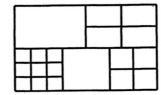

14. You have a photo that has been reduced to half the size of the original. What percent do you need to use now to produce an image 20% larger than the original?

15. The department store had a sale yesterday and they advertised 30% off marked prices on all winter coats. Today they said they would take off an additional 25%. If you buy a coat today, what percent will you be saving?

16. You start with a certain quantity and successive increases and decreases are performed on the quantity. On the result of your first action, another increase or decrease is performed. What percent of the original quantity will result?

a. A decrease of 20% is followed by an increase of 40%

b. An increase of 20% is followed by a decrease of 10%

c. A decrease of 20% is followed by an increase of 30%

d. An increase of 20% is followed by a decrease of 40%

e. A decrease of 30% is followed by an increase of 50%

17. Write a complete multiplication statement ($a \cdot b = c$) based on each of these models.

a.
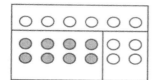

b.

c.

18. Use an area model for each problem.

a. $\dfrac{5}{6} \cdot \dfrac{2}{5}$

b. $\dfrac{1}{5} \div \dfrac{1}{3}$

c. $1\dfrac{1}{3} \cdot \dfrac{3}{4}$

d. $\dfrac{1}{3} \div \dfrac{1}{6}$

e. $1\dfrac{1}{8} \div \dfrac{2}{3}$

f. $2\dfrac{1}{2} \cdot \dfrac{4}{5}$

g. $1\dfrac{1}{4} \div \dfrac{5}{6}$

h. $2\dfrac{1}{2} \div \dfrac{1}{2}$

i. $1\dfrac{2}{3} \cdot \dfrac{4}{5}$

j. $\dfrac{3}{4} \div \dfrac{5}{8}$

19. For each problem, a) find the operator, and b) solve the problem.

a. Pat and Pam agree that a fair exchange is 3 apples for half a candy bar. If Pam gives Pat $3\dfrac{1}{2}$ candy bars, how many apples should he give her?

b. Pat and Pam agree that a fair trade is $1\frac{1}{4}$ pounds of rice for $\frac{1}{2}$ pound of sugar. If Pat gives Pam 5 pounds of rice, how much sugar should he give her?

c. Pat and Pam own livestock and they agree that a fair exchange is 2 cows for 9 sheep. If Pat has 26 sheep, how many cows can he expect to get from Pam?

20. A US dollar can be exchanged today for 108.275 Japanese Yen (JPY). If I exchange 5000 JPY for US dollars, how many dollars will I receive?

21. A Chilean Pesos (CLP) is worth .001579 US dollars. If I trade $300 US for pesos, how many CLP will I receive?

22. Fill in the missing information about this machine.

Input	Output
12	
	12
9	
	4
1	

23. Someone forgot to fill in the label on this machine. Here is some information about what this machine is doing. Please label the machine.

input	output
12 pieces	4 packages
18 pieces	6 packages
24 pieces	8 packages

24. Write the complete multiplication statement (a × b = c) that can be read from each model.

a.

b.

14

Rational Numbers as Measures

Discussion of Activities

1. a. By successively partitioning, you can see that you have about $\frac{23}{32}$ of a tank. Answers may vary due to accuracy in partitioning, but you should get a result close to .71.

   b. $\frac{7}{16}$ tank or close to .44

2. a. You have $\frac{10}{16}$ or $\frac{5}{8}$ of a gallon left.

   b. You bought 5 gallons.

   Because the tank holds 14 gallons, that is $\frac{5}{14}$ tank.

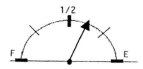

   c. By successively partitioning, you can see that you have about $\frac{3}{32}$ of a tank left. (Again, due to inaccuracy of partitioning, you may get a slightly different result, but it should be in the ball park of .09.) This means that you used $\frac{29}{32}$ of a tank, which was about 11 gallons of gas ($340 \div 31 = 10.967$). So if you divide the 11 gallons divided into 29 parts, then you would have $\frac{1}{32}$ of a tank, and 32 times that amount would be a full tank. $\frac{11}{29}$ (32) = 12.14 gallons.

3. a. By successive partitioning, get $\frac{23}{32}$ or 27 ounces.

   b. By successive partitioning, get $\frac{9}{16}$ or 18 ounces.

4.

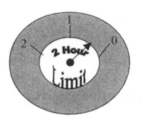

5. a. Divide your fractions. The resulting decimal numbers should be between .67 and .71 (or close to these).

   b. Divide your fractions. The resulting decimal numbers should be between .189 and .227 (or close to these).

6. a. Partition into 24^{ths}. The order is $\dfrac{5}{6}, \dfrac{21}{24}, \dfrac{11}{12}$.

   b. Partition into 18^{ths}. The order is $\dfrac{3}{9}, \dfrac{1}{2}, \dfrac{5}{6}$.

   c. Partition into 28^{ths}. The order is $\dfrac{6}{7}, \dfrac{13}{14}, \dfrac{27}{28}$.

7. **a.** $\dfrac{6}{9} = \dfrac{2}{3}$

   b. $\dfrac{9}{20}$

8. a. One full rotation means that 12 hours have elapsed.

   b. 1 hour of time

   c. 12 minutes or $\dfrac{1}{5}$ hour

9. a. One full rotation means that 1 hour has elapsed.

   b. 5 minutes

   c. 1 minute

10. Annie says that by dividing 7 by any number between 11 and 12, her fractions will remain between $\dfrac{7}{12}$ and $\dfrac{7}{11}$. To keep your fractions between $\dfrac{7}{9}$ and $\dfrac{7}{8}$, divide 7 by any number between 8 and 9, such as $8\dfrac{1}{2}, 8\dfrac{1}{3}, 8\dfrac{1}{4}$. Check your fractions by dividing. They should be greater than .77 and less than .875.

11. Jon thought of 12 as $11\dfrac{4}{4}$, then by dividing 7 by any number between $11\dfrac{0}{4}$ and $11\dfrac{4}{4}$, he could write a fraction between $\dfrac{7}{12}$ and $\dfrac{7}{11}$. To keep your fractions between $\dfrac{7}{9}$ and $\dfrac{7}{8}$, divide 7 by any number between $8\frac{0}{4}$ and $8\frac{4}{4}$, such as $8\frac{1}{4}$, $8\frac{1}{2}$, $8\frac{3}{4}$. Check your fractions by dividing. They should be greater than .77 and less than .875.

12. a. By partitioning the 2 hours into 16^{ths}, you can see that $\frac{7}{8}$ of an hour is left, which is $52\frac{1}{2}$ minutes.

 b. By partitioning 1 hour into 8^{ths} or 2 hours into 16^{ths}, you can see that $\frac{3}{8}$ of an hour or $\frac{3}{16}$ of 2 hours remains. This is $22\frac{1}{2}$ minutes.

Supplementary Activities

1. Use partitioning to find two fractions between those given.

    a. $\dfrac{1}{6}$ and $\dfrac{1}{5}$

    b. $\dfrac{9}{10}$ and 1

2. On the clock at the right, draw the location of the hour hand and the minute hand when the time is precisely 1:25. Explain how you knew where to point the hands.

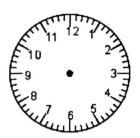

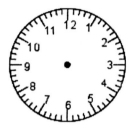

3. On the clock at the left, draw the locations of the hour and the minute hands when the time is 8:50.

4. The first gas meter shows how much gas you had before your trip and the seconds one shows how much you had when you got home. What part of a tank did you use for the trip? If your gas tank holds 16 gallons, how much gas did you use?

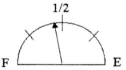
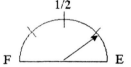

5. How much oil is left in each bottle?

    a.   b.

6. My book has 1004 pages and I am almost finished reading it. About how many pages have I read?

7. I have two stacks of $1000 bills. If the tall stack is worth $1 million, how much money is in the shorter stack? (Measure where the wrapper goes around the money.)

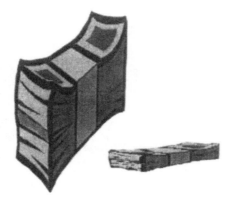

8. Tell how much time is left on each parking meter.

a.    b.

9. Parking downtown is expensive. The meters indicate that 1 nickel buys 3 minutes of time, for 1 dime you get 8 minutes, and for 1 quarter you get 20 minutes. You put in 2 nickels and 4 dimes. Draw an arrow to show how much time registers on the meter.

15

Ratios and Rates

Discussion of Activities

1. a. 2 boys:3 girls

b. The number of cows is $\frac{4}{5}$ the number of pigs, so the ratio of cows to pigs is 4:5.

c. The ratio of Mary's height to her mom's height is 2:3.

d. The ratio of Dan's weight to Becky's weight is 5:2.

2. a. $\frac{2}{7}$

b. 2:5

3. a. $\frac{80}{100}$

b. 30 balcony:70 floor

c. 20 empty:80 occupied

d. 20 empty:10 occupied in the balcony

4. a. The small gear makes $1\frac{3}{8}$ turns every time the large gear turns around once.

b. Then the small gear has made 5 turns, the large gear has made $3\frac{7}{11}$ turns.

c. 4 turns of the small gears use 32 teeth, so the large gear would need $32 \div \frac{4}{3}$ or 24 teeth.

d. 4 turns of the large gear would require 44 teeth, so the small gear would need $44 \div \frac{11}{3} = 12$ teeth.

5. A, C, and F are correct.

6. a. 3:4 is greater than 5:9 or you have a better chance of winning with the odds 3:4 than with the odds 5:9.

b. The picture shows that 3:4 = 15:20 and 5:9 = 15:27. This means that both ratios show 15 fors, but 5:9 has 7 more againsts.

c. $3(5:9) - 5(3:4) = (0:7)$

7. Other pictures are possible, depending on which fraction or ratio you clone.

    a. 11:12 is greater because, after removing copies of 5:6, we have 1:0. 11:12 − 2(5:6)
        = 1:0

    b. 12:16 and 3:4 are equivalent because cloning one produces the other. 4(3:4) = 12:16

    c. Cloning 5:8 and removing 5 copies of 7:9, we see that we get 0 for:11 against, so
        5:8 is less than 7:9. 7(5:8) − 5(7:9) = 0:11

    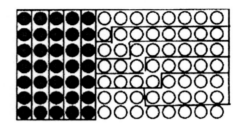

    d. Make 5 copies of $\frac{7}{8}$ and 4 copies of $\frac{9}{10}$. The clone of $\frac{7}{8}$ is $\frac{35}{40}$. Rearranging the clone

        of $\frac{9}{10}$, we can see that it is $\frac{36}{40}$. Therefore $\frac{9}{10} > \frac{7}{8}$.

    e. Make 9 copies of 7:8 and remove 7 copies of 9:10 to get 0:2.

    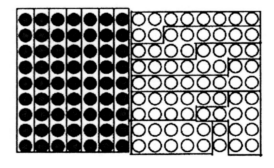

f. Clone $\dfrac{4}{9}$ and $\dfrac{3}{10}$ until there are 90 in each set. Rearrange the $\dfrac{4}{9}$ clone to get $\dfrac{40}{90}$ and compare to the $\dfrac{3}{10}$ clone, which is $\dfrac{27}{90}$. $\dfrac{4}{9} > \dfrac{3}{10}$.

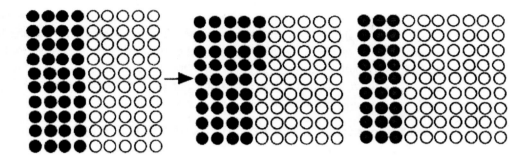

g. Removing copies of 4:5 from 8:15, we get 0:5. Therefore, 4:5 is larger. 8:15 − 2(4:5) = 0:5.

8. a. The ratio 3:6 is extendible over the people who are in the theater. Because the information about how many adults and how many children is already lost, we can further reduce this ratio, say, to 1:2.

   b. The ratio was not extendible, and not reducible without loss of information. We cannot add to or subtract teeth from a gear. The ratio of teeth on the small gear to the number of teeth on the large gear is 30:45. Writing the ratio as 2:3 gives up size of the gear.

   c. The ratio 12:14 is not extendible. We cannot add children to the classroom or increase the number of existing pets. In reducing the ratio, we lose the information about how many children are in the class.

   d. The ratio is not extendible. For example, if the perimeter is 24, the area is 36, not 18. The ratio is also not reducible without losing information.

   e. The ratio is extendible within the same bag of candies and to the extent that we don't go over the total number of pieces in the bag. The ratio is also reducible. For example, 3:6 = 1:2. Information about the number of candies has already been lost.

   f. The ratio is not extendible. It will not be true again that the ratio of the child's age to the mother's age will be 4:6. The ratio is reducible to 2:3 without loss of information, because 4:6 does not give us present ages.

   g. The ratio is not extendible. Dave will not be growing! If the ratio is reduced, we lose the information about both people's current heights.

   h. The ratio $2.6:4 oz. is extendible. We may assume that you can purchase more than 4 ounces at the same rate. The ratio is reducible to $.65 per ounce.

i. The ratio is not extendible. The family has only 6 children. If the ratio is reduced, we lose the information about how many children are in the family.

9. The ratios are realistically only approximations, but if we assume that they are exact and that the number of students is not changing, then the number of students has to be divisible by both 30 and 25 because we cannot hire fractions of teachers. $30 = 2 \cdot 3 \cdot 5$ and $25 = 5 \cdot 5$. So look at multiples of 150. If the school has 300 students, then it has 10 teachers, and $300{:}12 = 25{:}1$, so they would need to hire 2 more teachers. If the school has 450 students and 15 teachers, the $450{:}18$ gives the required ratio and they would need to hire 3 more teachers. Similarly, if the school has 600 students and 20 teachers, $600{:}24 = 25{:}1$, so they would need 4 more teachers. The number of teachers needed is approximately 1 for every 150 students.

10. Student A used a correct strategy. Notice that after removing one copy of 3:4 from 5:8, you are left with 2:4, which is less than 3:4. Student B used a correct strategy, but did not know how to interpret the result. Because there are 2 "against" dots remaining, 3:4 < 5:6. We get 0:2 and conclude that 5:6 > 2:3 although there were 3 copies of 5:6 and 5 copies of 3:4.

11. Charlie actually got the same deal as they offered at the Sweet Shop.

12. a. Looking at the ratios of money to people: $3(59{:}7) - 7(26{:}3) = (177{:}21) - (182{:}21) = (-5{:}0)$. This means that for the Golden Theatre, the money-to-people ratio is less, so the people-to-money ratio is more. Golden has the better price.

   b. Looking at win-to-loss ratios: $5(7{:}9) - 7(5{:}7) = (35{:}45) - (35{:}49) = (0{:}{-}4)$. This means that for the 7:9 record, the loss-to-win ratio is more, so the win-to-loss ratio is better. 7:9 is the better record.

   c. Looking at the seat-to-people ratios: $14(6{:}5) = 6(14{:}11) = (84{:}70) - (84{:}66) = (0{:}4)$. This means that for the car, the people-to-seats ratio is higher, so the seats-to-people ratio is lower and the car is more crowded.

13. JS made clones of $\frac{4}{6}$ and of $\frac{7}{9}$ until both clones had the same number of chips. When both had 18 chips, he could see that $\frac{14}{18}$, the clone of $\frac{7}{9}$, was greater than $\frac{12}{18}$, the clone of $\frac{4}{6}$.

Supplementary Problems

1. Translate these statements into ratio notation:

   a. Diet Zoom has $\frac{2}{3}$ fewer calories that the Regular Zoom Cola.

   b. Spritzer has $\frac{2}{3}$ as many calories as Splash.

   c. The nationally known brand is half again as expensive as the store brand.

   d. For every 2 crooks, there are 300 honest people.

2. Mr. Roberts sent 10 students into the meeting room where there were 6 seats at a large table and 2 small desks. He told them to sit down and wait for him. The boys took all of the seats and left all of the girls standing.

   a. What was the ratio of boys to girls?

   b. What fraction of the students had seats?

   c. What fraction of the students were girls?

   d. What was the ratio of students to seats?

3. Sunnybrook Academy reported that their student–teacher ratio was 11:1. The public school in the same area has 624 students.

   a. Why does Sunnybrook advertise the ratio 11:1 instead of reporting actual numbers of students and teachers?

   b. How many teachers would the public school need to keep up with the academy?

4. Steve compared 3:7 and 6:11 and his dot picture is shown.

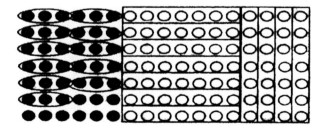

   a. What do the 9 uncircled black dots mean?

   b. Reinterpret the picture in terms of a ratio subtraction expressed symbolically.

5. Sandra wanted to compare $\frac{3}{4}$ and $\frac{5}{9}$. She did it by cloning both fractions.

    a. Show the dot picture she used and interpret it.

    b. Use the dot pictures to write a fraction equation showing the difference between the two fractions.

6. a. Show two different dot pictures comparing 3:4 and 5:9.

    b. For each of the pictures, express the difference between the ratios symbolically.

7. Using dot pictures, compare 5:7 and 8:11 two different ways, interpret each solution, and write the ratio subtraction symbolically.

8. Trent mixes chocolate milk every day after school. Yesterday he put 4 teaspoons of chocolate syrup into 6 ounces of milk. Today he put 3 teaspoons of chocolate into 4 ounces of milk. Which drink had the stronger chocolate flavor, yesterday's or today's?

9. Would you rather be taxed $15 on a purchase of $68 or $12 on a purchase of $52?

10. Stacy's offered a discount of 15% off on a purchase of $100 or more and Boss Store offered $20 off a $100 purchase. Which was the better discount?

11. The Lamplight Theater sold 50 tickets in two weeks, while the Globe sold 150 tickets in 4 weeks. At which theater are the tickets selling faster?

12. The Jones Company has a loss of $500 in 3 weeks, while the McDuff Company had a loss of $700 in 8 weeks. Which company suffered the least?

13. Which solution is stronger, 35 parts ammonia in 55 parts water, or 25 parts ammonia in 45 parts water?

14. Describe how one full turn of the yellow gear compares with one full turn of the red gear.

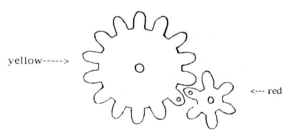

15. Here is Jennifer's work in which she compares $\frac{3}{4}$ and $\frac{5}{8}$. Is she correct?

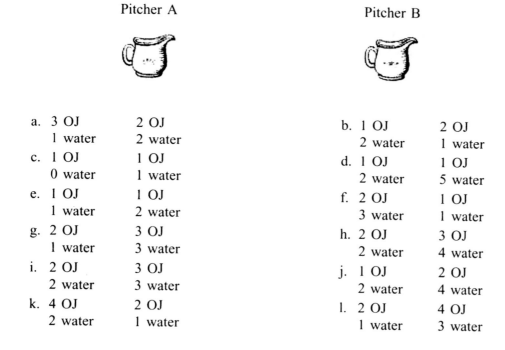

Dear Mrs.L,

I can do it two ways.

If I start with $\frac{3}{4}$ I make clones until I can get $\frac{5}{8}$ out of it.

$\frac{3}{4}$ is bigger. There is money left and all the people got in.

If I start with $\frac{5}{8}$ I make clones until I can get $\frac{3}{4}$ out of it.

$\frac{5}{8}$ is smaller. There is no money left and 4 people still need to get in.

I go until I use up one of the numbers.

Jennifer

16. You have 2 pitchers, A and B, and in each of them you mix up an orange juice concentrate and water recipe. For each pair of recipes below, decide which is going to have the stronger orange taste and be able to support your answer.

Pitcher A

Pitcher B

a. 3 OJ   2 OJ
    1 water   2 water

c. 1 OJ   1 OJ
    0 water   1 water

e. 1 OJ   1 OJ
    1 water   2 water

g. 2 OJ   3 OJ
    1 water   3 water

i. 2 OJ   3 OJ
    2 water   3 water

k. 4 OJ   2 OJ
    2 water   1 water

b. 1 OJ   2 OJ
    2 water   1 water

d. 1 OJ   1 OJ
    2 water   5 water

f. 2 OJ   1 OJ
    3 water   1 water

h. 2 OJ   3 OJ
    2 water   4 water

j. 1 OJ   2 OJ
    2 water   4 water

l. 2 OJ   4 OJ
    1 water   3 water

m.	1 OJ	2 OJ	n.	2 OJ	1 OJ
	3 water	5 water		3 water	2 water
o.	2 OJ	3 OJ	p.	6 OJ	5 OJ
	1 water	2 water		3 water	2 water
q.	4 OJ	5 OJ	r.	2 OJ	3 OJ
	2 water	3 water		3 water	4 water
s.	3 OJ	4 OJ	t.	5 OJ	7 OJ
	2 water	3 water		2 water	3 water

17. Analyze Nancy's response to this problem.

 eats  in 7 days.  eats ▨ ▨ ▨ ▨ in 4 days.

Who has bigger appetite, Slime Man or Snake Lady?

Nancy.

$3(5:7) - 5(3:4)$
$15:21 - 15:20 = 0:1$

No matter how many times you clone 5:7 and take 3:4 out of it, you are always going to have more days than you have food. So 3:4 must mean more food.

16

Distance-Rate-Time Relationships

Discussion of Activities

1. a. You are going 4 mph.

b. You traveled for $\frac{1}{4}$ hr.

c. You are going 21 mph.

d. It took you 12 minutes.

e. You are going 120 mph.

2. a. Find the total distance around the track (mi or km) covered by each driver by counting how many times he went around the divide by the time (3 hours) to get each driver's speed (mph or kph).

b. Time the drivers to see how long it took them to drive the 50 km and then divide that distance (km) by time (hours) to get km per hour.

3. You must be doing 72 miles per hour. It took you 50 sec to go 1 mile. That means you did .1 mi in 5 sec or 1.2 mi in 60 seconds (1 minute). Your hourly speed would then be 72 mph.

4. If it takes me 20 minutes (or $\frac{1}{3}$ hr) to get there at 40 mph, then the distance must be $\frac{40}{3}$ miles. $\frac{40}{3}$ at 50 mph will take about 16 minutes.

5. Both jets will get there at the same time. They both travel 1200 mph and will be there in 5.5 minutes.

6. $\frac{1}{5}$ mi. in 10 seconds = $\frac{1}{50}$ mi. per second = $\frac{60}{50}$ mi. per min. = $\frac{3600}{50}$ mi. per hour = 72 mph.

7. Jim can cut $\frac{1}{4}$ lawn in 1 hour. His brother can cut $\frac{1}{3}$ lawn in 1 hour. Working together, in 1 hour the boys can cut $\frac{1}{4}$ lawn + $\frac{1}{3}$ lawn = $\frac{7}{12}$ lawn. This means that they can cut $\frac{1}{12}$ lawn in $\frac{1}{7}$ hour, and the whole lawn in $\frac{12}{7}$ hours = $1\frac{5}{7}$ hours = 1 hour and 43 minutes.

8. There are 130 km between stations A and C. It took the train 2.25 times as long to go between B and C, so the distance must be 2.25 times as great as between A and B. The distance between B and C is 90 km.

9. At the rate of 13 parts per hour, worker 1 makes 117 parts in 9 hours. That means worker 2 made 126 parts in 9 hours or 14 parts per hour.

10. If your salary rose $2.50 per hour then stayed the same for 2 years, the total increase was $2.50 over 3 years. That is an average increase of $.83 per hour for the 3-year period.

11. a. The change is 24 miles in 29 minutes or $\frac{29}{60}$ hour. $24 \div \frac{29}{60} = 49.66$ mph.

    b. The change is 39 miles in 32 minutes, which is 73.13 mph.

    c. The change is 63 miles in 61 minutes which is 61.97 mph, or about 62 mph.

12. a. After 10 minutes, B was ahead of A and stayed in the lead throughout the hour. B was faster.

    b. In 60 minutes, B covered 6 miles. B's rate was 6 mph. A covered 2 miles in 6 minutes. A's rate was 2 mph.

    c. When you divide total distance covered by the total time it took, you get average speed. So 6 mph and 2 mph are average speeds. Typically, knowing an average speed does not tell us what rate a person was moving in any particular interval. They could be moving a little faster in one interval and a little slower in the next. However, in this case, because A's and B's positions in the sketch are in a straight line, we know that each kept the same pace throughout the 60 minutes.

13. a. 40 km in 3 hours = $13\frac{1}{3}$ kph.

    b. 20 km in 2 hours = 10 kph.

    c. 60 km in 5 hours = 12 kph.

14. Walking takes three times as long as traveling by bus. In 8 hours, there are 4 time periods, each 2 hours long, so we need 2 hours of time on the bus, and 6 hours (3 times as long) to walk back. Riding for 2 hours at the rate of 9 mph on the bus, we can go 18 miles.

15. Troy has to run 40 m at a speed of 3 meters per second. He can do it in $13\frac{1}{3}$ seconds.

    Tara has to run 100 m and at 5 meters per second. She can do it in 20 seconds. Tara will win the race.

Supplementary Problems

1. Suppose an object moves at a constant speed of 30 mph for $\frac{1}{2}$ hour.

   a. Graph the relationship between its speed and time.
   b. How far did the object go during this time period?
   c. Where can this distance be seen on your graph?

2. Suppose a body moves 50 feet in a straight line at a constant speed and it takes 4 seconds.

   a. What is its average speed during the 4 seconds?
   b. If we break down the 4-second time interval into seconds, it may not be the case that the object moved the same distance in each of those subintervals. For example, suppose we know that this object moved 10 feet in the first second, 10 feet in the second second, 20 feet in the third second, and 10 feet in the fourth second. What was the average speed during sec_1, sec_2, sec_3, sec_4?
   c. Graph speed as a function of time from 0–4 seconds.

3. The activity of each of five people in their cars over a 6-hour period is recorded on these graphs. Tell what each person did.

   a.
   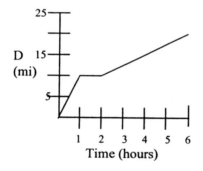

   b.
   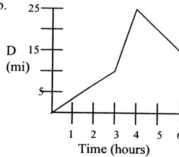

   c.
   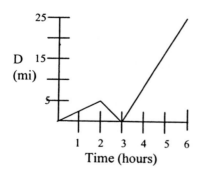

   d.
   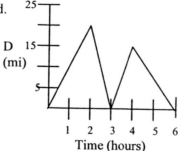

e.

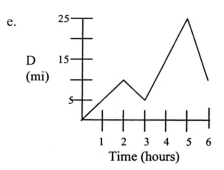

4. The following graphs show people's activity over a time period of 30 seconds. When possible, describe what each person is doing. If a graph does not make sense, tell why.

a.   b.   c.

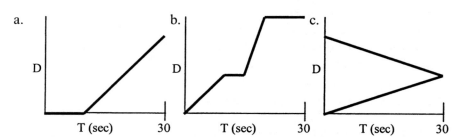

d.   e.   f.

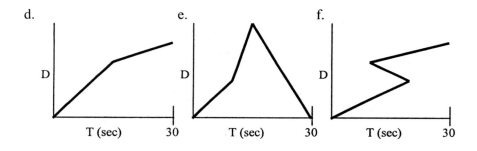

g.   h.   i.

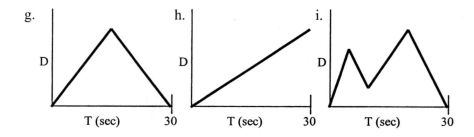

5. Sketch graphs showing the following information.

   a. A car drives at a speed of 40 mph for 3 hours and then in the same direction at a speed of 60 mph for 2 hours.

   b. A car drives for 1 hour at a speed of 50 mph then turns around and drives home at the speed of 40 mph.

6. Bill drove 380 miles in 6 hours and Greg drove 130 miles in 2 hours.

   a. Compare these rates by finding their unit rates.

   b. Which would appear as the steeper line on a graph?

7.

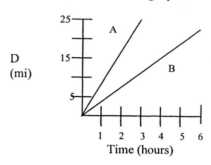

   a. Which car is faster?

   b. How much faster?

8.

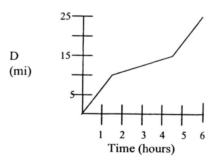

   a. How fast was this car moving during the first segment of its trip?

   b. During the second segment?

   c. During the third segment?

   d. What was its average speed for this 6-hour trip?

   e. Graph the average speed on the graph given above.

9. You drive at a speed of 35 mph for 15 minutes, then walk back to your origin at a speed of 4 mph. What is your average speed for this trip?

10. Sketch a graph that shows your activity.

   a. You run as fast as you can for 5 seconds, rest for 5 seconds, then walk for 20 seconds.

   b. You walk for 10 seconds, run as fast as you can for 10 seconds, and then turn around and walk back toward your starting point for 10 seconds.

    c. You walk for 10 seconds, turn around and walk back to where you started in five seconds, and then run as fast as you can away from your starting point for 15 seconds.

    d. You walk for 5 seconds, run for 5 seconds, walk for 5 seconds, run for 5 seconds, and so on until 30 seconds are up.

    e. You walk for 15 seconds, turn around and walk toward your starting point for 5 seconds, then turn and walk away from the starting point again and walk for 10 seconds.

11. You drive for 3 hours at a speed of 55 mph then you slow down and drive for 2 hours at 40 mph. What is your average speed for this trip?

12. A car's journey is depicted in this graph.
    a. What was its speed during the first 2 hours?
    b. What was it speed during the next 4 hours?
    c. What was its average speed for the 6-hour trip?
    d. On the same graph, show what the car's journey would have looked had it traveled at a constant speed for the whole journey.

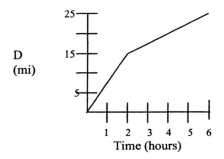

13. Using the following graph, answer these questions:
    a. What is the speed of car A?
    b. What is the speed of car B?
    c. What do parallel lines indicate about speed on a distance-time graph?
    d. Why do the graphs not coincide? What is the difference between the two journeys?

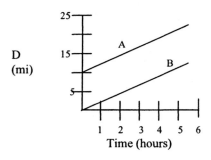

14. Use the following graph to answer these questions:
   a. What is the speed of car A?
   b. What is the speed of car B?
   c. What does the intersection point mean?

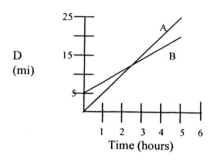

15. Charlie got a traffic ticket for a moving violation: traveling 5 mph over the 55 mph speed limit. The officer's citation said that he followed Charlie for 10 miles and that he averaged 60 mph, which was 5 mph over the speed limit. Charlie drove at 80 mph for the first 5 miles and then at 40 mph for the next 5 miles. Charlie went to traffic court. How did he argue his case?

16. Frank drove from Boston to Washington and back again. He averaged 50 mph on the way and 60 mph on the way back. The round trip took him 18 hours. How far apart are the two cities?

17. A cruise ship headed out for a trans-Atlantic trip traveling at a constant speed of 25 knots. A passenger who missed the departure hired a speedboat to catch up. The speedboat traveled at 45 knots. The speedboat left the dock precisely 2 hours after the cruise ship did. How far from the dock were the two boats when they met?

18. Frank and Flo have a pet fly named Frieda, who can not stand it when the twins are separated, so she flies back and forth between them at a rapid rate of 50 mph. Frank was downtown and Flo was at home—distance of 10 miles apart—when they both hopped on their biked and sped along their secret path towards each other. Each was going 20 mph. Frieda Fly started on Frank's handlebars and flew along the path to Flo's handlebars, and then back to Frank's, then back to Flo's, until the twins met each other on the path. How far did Frieda travel?

19. Frieda Fly has a twin who Frank and Flo named Free-To. Free-To Fly looks like Frieda Fly, but he travels at a different rate—15 km per hour. Once when Frank and Flo were 9 km apart on their bikes, Free-To was upset and traveled along their path between them until they met. Frank was traveling eastbound at a speed of 10 mph and Flo was traveling westbound at 8 mph.
   a. How long did it take Frank and Flo to meet?
   b. How far did Free-To Fly travel by the time Frank and Flo met.

20. Are these rates the same? Explain.

    a. $3 per pound and 3 pounds per dollar.

    b. 3 meters per second and 3 seconds per meter.

21. I ran the mile in 10 minutes. How far did I run in 1 minute? What was my speed in miles per hour?

22. An empty canoe that was not tied down floated down the river, going 7 miles in $1\frac{1}{2}$ hours. What was the speed of the current?

23. A boy can bike a mile in 5 minutes and walk a mile in 20 minutes. How much time does he save if he bikes to his dad's office, 8 miles away, rather than walking?

24. Mike drove for 3 hours and traveled 110 miles. Then he got a flat and had to walk the rest of the way to his destination. He walked the last 11 miles in 2.5 hours.

    a. What was his average speed on the first part of the trip?

    b. What was his average speed on the second part of the trip?

    c. What was his average speed for the whole journey?

25. A biker rides at a speed of 10 mph for about half an hour and then turns around and walks home on the same route, at a speed of 4 miles per hour. What is his average speed for the entire trip?

26. Carrie climbed Crow's Peak at the rate of $1\frac{1}{2}$ miles per hour and came down at the rate of $4\frac{1}{2}$ miles per hour. It took her 6 hours to travel both ways.

    a. How far is the top of the peak?

    b. How long did it take her to get down?

27. Jim and Ken are brothers and they are both on the track team. They frequently race each other in practice, giving Jim a bit of an advantage because he is younger and his best speed is only 3 meters per second. Ken runs 5 meters per second. This week, they ran a 150-meter race, and Ken gave Jim a 30-meter head start. Which brother won the race? How far into the race did he pass the loser?

28. A shoe company sells 500 pairs of shoes a day if the price is $46 a pair and 430 pairs a day if the price is $54 a pair. What is the rate of change of sales with respect to price?

29. A bus travels 2 miles uphill and its average speed on the way up is 25 mph. At what speed would it have to travel down the hill so that the average speed for the entire trip is 40 mph?

30. Compare these rates by finding the constants associated with their equivalence classes.

    a. 30 heartbeats per 15 seconds; 64 heartbeats in 30 seconds.

    b. a loss of 30 pounds in 7 months; a loss of 8 pounds in 6 weeks.

31. Marcia graphed the amount of water (vertical scale) against the amount of sugar (horizontal scale) in each of 3 lemonade recipes. The line for recipe C turned out to be the steepest, and the line for recipe B, the flattest.

a. Which recipe tasted sweetest?

b. How would you interpret a horizontal line in this situation?

32. As the cold front gripped the city, the temperature dropped rapidly. Between 4 and 5 pm, the temperature fell 10 degrees. Between 5 and 6 pm, the temperature fell 8 degrees. Between 6 and 7 pm, the temperature fell 6 degrees. Between 7 and 8 pm, the temperature fell 7 degrees.

a. How much did the temperature drop between 4 and 6 pm?

b. What was the average rate of change between 4 and 6 pm?

c. What is the difference between the information given by your answer for a and your answer for b?

d. What was the average rate of change between 6 and 8 pm?

e. What was the average rate of change between 4 and 8 pm?

f. Why are your answers for b, d, and e all different?

33. When the lights went out, my mother looked for some candles. She found two pillars of the same diameter, but one was $1\frac{1}{2}''$ shorter than the other. She lit the taller one at 8 pm, and the shorter at 9 pm. At 10:30 pm, both candles were the same height. At midnight, the candle that was originally shorter burned out. At 12:30, the other candle burned out. Assuming that the candles burned at constant rates, how tall was each candle originally?

17

Similarity and Percents

Discussion of Activities

1. Look at the longer side of the rectangle as compared to the longer side of the paper. $2 \cdot (5.5) = 11$. If I use a scale factor of 5.5 on the other side of the rectangle, I get $(1.5) \cdot (5.5) = 8.25$. So, the largest similar rectangle will have dimensions 8.25" by 11" and the scale factor that gives it is 5.5.

2. If $2\frac{1}{2}'$ is $\frac{1}{20}$ of the actual size, then the height of the actual dinosaur used in the movie was $20 \cdot \left(2\frac{1}{2}\right) = 50'$.

3. The area of A may be calculated like this: top piece of 2 sq units + bottom piece of 8 sq units = 10 sq units. The area of B is then 8 sq units in the top + 32 sq units in the bottom = 40 sq units. Therefore, the area of A has been increased by a factor of 4 in figure B by doubling the lengths of the sides.

4. a. the scale model of the tennis court should measure 6 cm by 11.5 cm
   b. the scale model of the sheet of paper should measure 2.5 mm by 4.5 mm
   c. the scale model of the desktop should measure 17.5 mm by 11 mm

7. The scale factor is $\frac{1}{2}$.

8. A, C, E, and G are similar. B, H, and I are similar. D and F are similar. J is not similar to any of the others. One way to decide which are similar is to compare the height to width ratios of the figures.

9. If you put the right angle of each triangle at the origin (0,0) with one side along the y axis and one side along the x axis, then the third sides of similar triangles should be parallel.

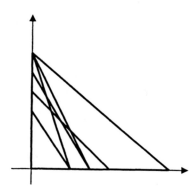

It appears that none of the triangles are similar and this can be confirmed by checking the ratios of corresponding sides.

10. a. The side of the smaller square is $\frac{1}{4}$ the side of the larger.

b. The scale factor is $\frac{1}{4}$.

11. a. B is an enlargement of A.

b. The scale factor is $\frac{3}{2}$ because every length on figure A is $1\frac{1}{2}$ times as long on figure B.

c. Right angles were preserved.

d. Vertical segments became $1\frac{1}{2}$ times as long on B as they were on A.

e. Horizontal segments became $1\frac{1}{2}$ times as long on B as they were on A.

f. The area of B is $\frac{9}{4}$ times the area of A.

g. The ratio of corresponding lengths is $\frac{3}{2}$.

h. Shrinking and enlarging preserves angles. Shrinking or enlarging multiplies each length by the scale factor and each area by the scale factor squared.

12. Compare the areas to the prices of the pizzas.

area (sq. in.)	price
78.54	$6.80
113.1	8.50
153.94	13.60
314.16	28.00

a. Compare price to number of square inches. For the 10″ pizza, you pay $.086 a square inch; for the 12″ pizza, $.075 a square inch; for the 14″ pizza, $.088 a square inch; for the 20″ pizza, $.089 a square inch. The 12″ pizza is the best buy.

b. No. The pizzas are not priced proportionally. For example, 78.54 sq. in. doubled is less than 153.94 sq. in., but the price for 153.94 sq. in. is double the price for 78.54 sq. in.

13. If the height to width ratio were 1:1, then you would have squares and all squares are similar.

14. a. The original mast must have been $(2.5)(14) = 35'$ tall

b. The original fish must have been $80(\frac{1}{25}) = 3.2$ feet long.

c. The original area must have been $(25)(\frac{1}{4.5})(\frac{1}{4.5}) = 1.235$ sq. ft.

15. a. 25% of 80 = 20

b. 15 = 30% of 50

c. 45 = 75% of 60

d. 14 = 20% of 70

e. 65% of 90 = 58.5

f. 28 = 40% of 70

g. 15% of 80 = 12

h. 36 is 40% of 90

i. 27 is 45% of 60

16. The markup is the amount of money the bookstore charges the student above and beyond what the store paid for the book. The equation says that the cost to the bookstore is $\frac{3}{4}$ what the student pays ($C = \frac{3}{4}$ S). This means that the student pays $\frac{4}{3}$ times the cost to the bookstore. So the markup is $\frac{1}{3}$ the cost to the bookstore or $33\frac{1}{3}$%.

17. a. If there were 100 questions, 80% would be 80 questions, so if there are only 50 questions, 80% is 40 correct.

b. 10% would be $1,500, so 5% is $750.

c. 1% would be $18, so 8% would be 8 times as much, or $144.

d. 10% is 20 pounds and 5% is 10 pounds, so the 15% that is not water weighs 30 pounds. The water must weigh 170 pounds.

18. To make an enlargement, each dimension must increase by the same factor. 3.5(2.429) = 8.5″, but 5″(2) = 10″. You cannot increase both dimensions by the same factor.

Supplementary Activities

1. This puzzle is not full size, but it is drawn to scale. Either on your computer or using a metric ruler on paper,

   a. create a full-size similar puzzle in which the 6 cm segment is only 4 cm long, and

   b. create a similar puzzle in which the 6 cm segment is 7 cm long.

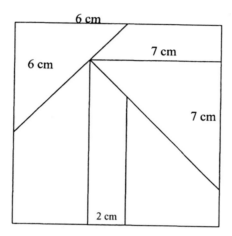

2. Are these figures similar? Explain.

3. The edge of this cube has been multiplied by 2.

   a. What happens to the area of the cube?

   b. What happens to the surface area of 1 face of the cube?

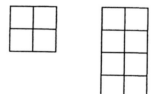

4. What happens to the area of a circle if you double its radius? Triple it?

5. The perimeter of this figure is 14 units. If I scale the figure by a factor of 3, what happens to the perimeter?

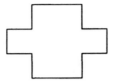

6. Suppose I enlarge this rectangle by a scale factor of 1.5, then I enlarge the resulting rectangle by a scale factor of 1.5, then I enlarge the new rectangle again by a scale factor of 1.5. What scale factor describes the relationship between this rectangle and the result of all my enlargements? What happens if I repeated this process ten times?

7. Use a ratio table to solve each of the following problems:
   a. ? is 62% of 30
   b. 136% of 80 = ?
   c. 57% of 29 = ?
   d. 23 is 15% of ?
   d. 42 is 36% of ?
   e. 26 is _____% of 74 (to two decimal places).

8. The following rectangles are similar. Find the missing measurement on the smaller rectangle.

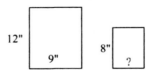

9. If two rectangles where congruent (that is, they have the same size and shape), what would be the relationship between their widths?

10. These letters are the same shape, but a different size. How long is the curve marked x?

11. a. What is the scale factor when a 2″ square is enlarged to become a 6″ square?

b. By what factor is its area enlarged?

12. Marvin wants to buy his mother a book for her birthday. It usually sells for $15.95, but during a special promotion, every bookstore he knew had a sale! Where did he buy it? At store A, the book is 5% off; at B it is $.50 off; at C it is $.50 off on the dollar; at D it is $\frac{1}{5}$ off; and at E it is 50% off.

13. Mike sold his cat to Kathy at a 10% loss. Later, she sold it back to him at a 10% gain. How does Mike do in the end? What percent profit of loss did he realize?

14. In your favorite department at Boss Store, you find a clearance rack that is marked "35% Off Already Discounted Prices." The skirt you want to buy was originally $49.99 and the ticket now says $39.99. How much will you pay, and what percent discount are you actually getting?

15. A package of paper weighs 3 pounds. What will be the weight of a package containing the same number of sheets and the same quality of paper with sheets that are twice as long and twice as wide as the sheets in the first package?

Challenging Problems

1. Roxie and her dad went on a hiking trip together on Morecrest Mountain. She carried the supplies $\frac{1}{3}$ of the way up and $\frac{3}{5}$ of the way down. If she carried the supply pack a distance of $17\frac{1}{2}$ miles, how far did they hike up the mountain?

2. In class yesterday, Professor Fracto noticed that $\frac{3}{4}$ of his students were female and there were 6 people absent. When he checked his records, he found that $\frac{2}{3}$ of those enrolled were female. Has there been a mistake?

3. A group of friends ate a bag of pistachios in one sitting, leaving just one nut in the bowl for me. They did not worry about dividing the nuts equally among themselves because there were too busy chatting and some like pistachios more than do others. Mandy took $\frac{2}{7}$ of them and Trish, $\frac{1}{12}$ of them. Alison and Kristen ate $\frac{1}{6}$ and $\frac{1}{3}$ respectively. Carol took 20, Kate took 12, and Pam, who was so busy talking that she forgot to eat, took 11 with her when she left. How many nuts were in the bowl before the girls got to them?

4. Solve this puzzle. It is time for bed. One fifth of three-eighths of what remains of the morning has already gone by. What time is it (to the nearest second)?

5. A man died and left to his elder son the task of splitting the five large bills, his lifetime savings. The son gave his brother twice two-thirds of his own share, and his mother $\frac{2}{8}$ of the younger brother's share. What fraction of the money did each receive?

6. Jim's wife had a baby yesterday morning. When the baby was born, the time until 12 noon was six times $\frac{2}{7}$ of the time since midnight. At what time was the baby born?

7. Oscar, Harvey, and Merv each have huge collections of pennies. One day they decided to weigh them. Oscar discovered that his collection outweighed Harvey's by $\frac{1}{3}$ of Merv's. Harvey's was the weight of Merv's plus $\frac{1}{3}$ of Oscar's. Merv's collection

weighted 10 pounds more than $\frac{1}{3}$ of Harvey's. How many pounds of pennies did each boy have?

8. Last Christmas, Mr. Moore gave each of his six daughters a box of a different weight, the lightest for the youngest, and so on until the heaviest went to the oldest daughter. Each box was one ounce heavier that the previous. If the sum of the weights was 6 pounds, what were the 6 weights?

9. Before he ended his life, the man who is buried here composed the inscription for his grave marker so that you could figure out the age at which he died. How old was he?

Here lies
Di O'Phantus

He was a boy for $\frac{1}{6}$ of his life, and $\frac{1}{12}$ of his life later, became an adult. After $\frac{1}{7}$ of his life, he married and 5 years later had a son. At only half his father's age, his son became ill and died. After trying to console himself for 4 years, he died with a broken heart.

10. A certain sculpture was made using 60 pounds of four different metals. The gold and bronze together accounted for $\frac{2}{3}$ of its weight. The gold and tin together comprised $\frac{3}{4}$ of its weight. The gold and iron together weighed 36 pounds. How much of each metal was used?

11. A man left this will. What was the dead man's fortune?

I leave my son $\frac{1}{5}$ of my wealth, and my wife $\frac{1}{12}$. I leave to each of my four grandsons, my two brothers, and my grieving mother, $\frac{1}{11}$ of my property. To my cousins, I leave $12,000 to share and to my friend Tom, $5,000. To my faithful employees I leave the following bonuses for their service: Ann, $350; Mark, $350; Steve, $600; Ray, $300; the delivery man, $200; the janitor, $200. It is my wish that $25,000 be spent on my mausoleum. Use $9,000 to cover the other costs associated with a modest funeral.

12. When my brother and I added the mileage we did on our bikes, we got 20 miles. If you add a third of my distance and a fourth of my brother's, you get 6 miles, the distance our mother cycled. How far did I go? How far did my brother go?

13. On Thursday night at the Larson household, each person gets home at a different time. Mike was home first. He skipped dinner, opened a bag of candy bars, and ate 6 of them. Alison came home next and helped herself to $\frac{1}{3}$ of the original contents of the bag. Mark got home just before Jenny and had $\frac{1}{2}$ of the remaining candy bars for his dessert. Jenny finished off the last two candy bars. Later, when Mrs. Larson got home and asked who ate the candy bars, Alison, the youngest, got blamed for eating most of the bag. For being so inconsiderate, she had to use her own money to buy a new bag of candy bars. Was this fair?

14. The Belly Jean Company sells purple passion jelly beans for $1.25 a pound and pink pineapple jelly beans for $1.85 a pound. How many pounds of purple must be added to 50 pounds of the pink jelly beans to create a mixture that sells for $1.45 a pound?

15. A man was stranded on a desert island with enough water to last him 27 days. After 3 days, he saved a woman on a small life raft. If they can keep their water supply from evaporating, they figure that they can share their water equally for 18 days. What portion of the man's original daily ration was allotted to the woman?

16. In a certain scout troop, 70% of the scouts had a compass, 75% had matches, 85% had a knife, and 85% had a watch. What percent of the scouts had all four pieces of equipment?

17. At a recent foxhunt, Prince Charles timed his favorite hound and found that he was running 10 m for every 6 m run by the fox. At one point, a fox was 30 m ahead of the hound. How far did the hound have to run to catch up with the fox?

18. Did you ever walk the steps of a moving escalator? In my favorite department store, I found that if I walk down 26 steps, I can get to the bottom in 30 seconds, and if I walk down 34 steps, I can get to the bottom in 18 seconds. How many steps are in the moving stairway? (Time is measured from the moment the first step beings to descend until I step on to the solid platform at the bottom.)